THE RANGE OF FAITH

THE RANGE OF FAITH

Basic Questions
for a Living Theology

Tony Kelly CSSR

THE LITURGICAL PRESS
Collegeville, Minnesota

Cover design by Mary Pauly.

Printed in the United States of America.

1	2	3	4	5	6	7	8	9

Library of Congress Cataloging-in-Publicata Data

Kelly, Tony.
   The range of faith : basic questions for a living theology / Tony Kelly.
      p. cm.
   Bibliography: p.
   ISBN 0-8146-1792-1
   1. Catholic Church—Doctrines. 2. Theology, Doctrinal.
I. Title.
BX1751.2.K39 1989   89-36072
230′.2—dc20   CIP

Contents

Foreword

I think the title of this book, *The Range of Faith,* pretty well sums up its contents, both in scope and style. For it does range far and wide in terms of the questions it considers. Though I have something to say, apparently, on everything from the Trinity to heaven, from marriage to purgatory, I am not intending to write another SUMMA. Though these various essays fall into fairly neat sequence, it remains that they were written, and usually published in some form[1], in response to demands as they occurred. You will notice that the big themes of theology keep reappearing: the nature of theology itself and its relationship to human experience; the Mystery of God; and the especially modern quest for freedom: liberation from the evils we suffer (and inflict on each other), freedom for the ultimate fulfilment of life in Christ; the meaning of belonging to the Church as a Catholic today.

It is my hope that it will provide some interesting, perhaps even inspiring approaches to these great realities, but also be an example of the task confronting modern Christian theology, while indicating something of its method in giving an account of our faith and hope.

The great theologians of South America have reminded us forcefully that the expression of faith is most genuine when it is intent on promoting human freedom and resisting everything that does violence to our humanity. I would like to think that this book is, in another context, an example of a 'free-thinking' (in the sense of 'freedom-promoting' theology). For an essential liberation for faith is one of mind. We believers must be freed to express our faith in a wonderful and inspiring way, even as the familiar evils of our age all but overwhelm us. This means being free to enter into a conversation with all the men and women of good will who are searching and struggling for hope. We cannot be defensively rigid. Faced with the complexity of our times, it is a temptation to become so, in the pretence of hiding behind some fixed and final formula. The great Henri de Lubac's words about reactionary thinkers are still worth pondering: 'They thought they belonged to eternity because they were not of their time.'

I think we need to keep the conversation going within the context of our time and culture. Above all, I think we need to keep speaking about the utterly essential, fundamental things. Once theology ceases to be an "introductio in mysterium" (leading into the mystery of God) it so easily becomes a "reductio ad absurdum", in which only the fanatic and the dilettante thrive. Ernest Becker said something wise when, in the course of writing his great book *The Denial of Death,* he noted, "Today we need simple-mindedness in order to be able to say anything at all." (p. 208) Theology is, in its ultimate and universal concerns, an attempt at such a simple mindedness. At least, I hope my efforts are.

But it is an adventure, this theological enterprise; and perhaps a sublime form of art, for its aim is the beautiful as well as the ultimate Truth and the universal Good. Christopher Fry's noble words have become quite emblematic for a lot of us involved in the teaching and learning of theology:

> Thank God our time is now
> When wrong comes up to face us everywhere.
> Never to leave us till we take
> the longest stride of soul man ever took.
> Affairs are now soul-size,
> The enterprise
> Is exploration into God.

> (From *The Sleep of Prisoners*)

So, "The Range of Faith" — faith reaching to its centre in the Trinity itself; love impatient with lesser versions of this God and the life we are offered; hope blossoming to proportions that are both worthy of God and resistant to the routine despairs that threaten us.   Tony Kelly, CSSR.

1. Usually in *Compass Theology Review, National Outlook* or the *Australasian Catholic Record.*

1

The expression of theology

MODERN theology knows its own kind of complications. Amongst theologians, there is such a diversity of styles, thought patterns, aims and emphases, that confusion often reigns. The confusion is doubly or triply compounded when the explicit context of theology nowadays is ecumenical and inter-faith. How, then, can we make sense of what theology is saying? And more pertinently, how can professional or amateur theologians know what they are doing? How can a contemporary faith come to expression?

The usual answer is this: we can speak by analogy. This is the general, and I believe, the accurate answer. Through our immediate experience and understanding of our world, we can speak of deeper mysteries. We can, and we do. By our experience of the solidity and permanence of a rock, or of the breadth and power of the ocean, we can speak of God as a rock or an ocean. This is, of course, metaphor, often called the "analogy of improper proportion". By our experience of persons, friends, community, we come to speak of God as a person, a friend, a father, a lover, or even love itself. This is a more real type of language. God is personal in a way that he is not a rock! This more real way of speech is usually called the "analogy of proper proportion", or the "analogy of attribution".

This is a serviceable answer, but it is not as simple as it seems. People have lived, and continue to live in a variety of societies and cultures. What is a true analogy for me, a moderately educated twentieth century Australian of vaguely European background, is hardly appropriate to a Hindu, a

Thai Buddhist or an Eskimo. It might not be so clear to these why God should be called personal, even why he should be "he" at all. Other cultures live in and from another world of experience, each with its own kind of "feel" for reality, shaped by its history, its language, its (at least implied) philosophy. Further, a new technological society has complicated our natural analogies even more. The obvious beauties of nature are not so readily available. Urban life cuts us off from them. Modern economics can destroy them. Modern advertising deadens our reactions by its absurd and trivial association of mountains and rivers, rolling plains and open skies with cigarettes, soap, automobiles and hair-spray. The images of family are eroded by the facts and myths of overpopulation, as images and associations of rural peace and plenty are complicated by a vast mechanization, and the caprices of the supply-demand patterns of huge economies.

Analogy, like all simple speech, has become enormously complicated.

Symbols

Yet, SYMBOLS do remain. They are the stuff of our total and vital expressiveness. They have their own ecumenism and universality. Symbols of light, human communication, sexual love reach far beyond any one culture. This is a world of investigation in itself.[1] Whether our natural symbols derive from our experience of the desert, of the cycles of fertility, of space travel, or from simply having lived in a "Lucky Country", they will shape our theology; and they will shape it firmly in one direction. Hence, a clue to much theological expression is given from the often unconscious influence of certain dominant symbols. Symbols do form a theology. Indeed, Paul Ricoeur has called them, "occasions for thinking". There is no thinking, unless we have what Aquinas long ago, called "converting to the phantasm". What are our dominant symbols? What is the character of our imaginative life? Good questions for any theologians, especially for those who think they can do without the symbolic, or imagine that they operate

10

beyond it. Good questions too for any theology that suddenly feels it has become parched and arid, with a loss of flair and inspiration.

Symbols, indeed, remain. Just as unnoticed, and for that reason very often neglected, the STORY also remains. Narrative remains as the fundamental dynamic category of theology.[2] Before theology can go on to analyse, discern and mould the judgements of our faith into a comprehensive whole, it must first tell a story. If this narrative quality is unrecognised, or dismissed as marginal, theology can so easily become divorced from the reality of history. For all stories have an engaging power about them to involve us, and speak to the deeper levels of our experience. As J. R. R. Tolkien has pointed out, the humble fairy story is the most real form of narrative. It relates the experience of living as "surprised by grace" (to use the phrase of another great storyteller, C. S. Lewis). Such stories are our introduction to the Gospel: for the Gospel is the archetype of all stories that deal with the "good catastrophies" of life, and reveal, in our very experience of evil, the surprise of redeeming grace.[3]

So, before theology forms any categories, or refines any of its expressions, it must recognize two things. The first, that symbols are the vital foundation of all reflection, moulding our outlook and shaping our horizon. The second, that the story, the narrative form, is the irreplaceable dynamic pattern underlying all our experience of God. If the Gospel is the "greatest story ever told", it is this because it so totally engages us in the whole drama and promise of human existence. The listeners are "drawn in" to experience the events therein narrated. The more usual name for this "being-drawn-in" is faith. The symbol and the narrative are the two absolutely *given* forms as far as theology is concerned. These remain the undercurrent of all theological endeavour. Theology thinks out its positions and its concepts only to return to this primary simplicity with a greater commitment and maturity.

Yet there are formal, analytical categories. Instead of being given to theology, they are critically elaborated and expressed.

Basic Categories

There are two basic categories that theology must concern itself with.[4] The first it has in common with every human science. It is shaped by the force of a simple question: how do I speak to human beings? Theology, after all, is for human beings, not for archangels on retreat. It must have a frame of reference that touches the human in all cultures and in all ages, since it serves the universal Word of God coming into the totality of human history. So, first of all, theology must express itself, in human terms, in the way we experience ourselves, consciously. We all experience something; all ask questions; all reflect; all make decisions. In brief, we all have a structure of consciousness that is not only common to all human cultures, but their foundation. In the measure they attend to their experiences, ask the right questions, reflect on the right answers, and give themselves to their right decisions, cultures progress and human life succeeds. At each level and phase of this consciousness, the question of an ultimate is posed. What am I finally experiencing? What is the final kind of intelligence? What is the ultimate truth? Before whom do I ultimately stand?

Hence, the structure of human conscious existence is the first basic general category. Since theology aims to speak in terms of what human fulfilment really is, it shapes itself according to the structure of human consciousness itself. This is at once dynamic and open. It bases itself not on Aristotelian or Platonic philosophy, not even on existentialism or personalism, not on the words of any master, but most securely on human being itself.

The second general category is shaped by this question: what is man experiencing in his religious existence? How do I speak to the religious person? This question is likewise imperative. "God wishes all men to be saved and to come to the knowledge of the truth". Presumably he has not been inactive in this regard. Our questions have found fundamental answers. Our pilgrimage has not been in vain. We do come to acknowledge an Absolute. We do come to stand before something or someone, who or which we may name "God". We come to a point of an ultimate concern, and even love, to a point of surrender and final hope. And this brings forth the fruits of love and peace, even joy and the dedicated service of others.

So it is that the second basic general category to form the expression of theology is the religious experience. This too is a universal category, not restricted to any age or culture.

So we can say that being-human and being-religious are the two basic categories. As an open style of thought, theology is based on a transcultural reality, human beings and their quest for an absolute fulfilment.

Besides general categories, there are the more easily recognized special categories of theological expression. Five are clearly necessary:

a. *Individual:* These deal with the individual experience of faith-hope-charity. Whether you talk about Jesus or Mary, Peter or Paul, Luther or Kierkegaard, Newman or Dorothy Day, theology is expected to resonate with what goes on in the hearts of individuals as each searches for God and finds him. This makes demands on the theologian. His own religious life might be so undeveloped that he cannot appreciate the religious worth of other people's lives. In that case he might be better advised to edit texts and work (as a labourer) on archaeological sites.

b. *Communitarian:* The faith-hope-charity of the individual is housed in the historical and social life of a community. The categories of community, Church, tradition, structure and office, charism and creed become necessary. Individuals are born out of a community. They are formed by it, sustained by it, and in turn form it.

c. *Originative:* If special categories deal with the religious development of individuals and their communities, a basic special category concerns itself with naming *the source* of such a development. The general Christian answer brings in here God named as Father, Son and Holy Spirit. Such a source is named not only as the ultimate cause but as the goal and end of religious development.

d. *Dialectic:* Theology, then, must develop categories to

express the religious development of individuals and communities as they are affected by the Mystery of God. Yet the task is not simple. For even theologians live in the midst of human ambiguities. Criteria must be devised and expressed. With these, we begin to discern the reality of life in the Spirit from enthusiasm, pietism, legalism, dogmatism and so forth. Such are the categories of dialectic and discernment.

e. *Redemptional:* Since theology deals with the entry of the real God into man's making of man, it must develop expressions to signify the fact and manner of God's undoing of human evil. It must be able to express how God offers our world a liberation from personal and collective decline for a genuine human progress. Theology must concern itself not only with the ongoing human development, but with the redemption from sin, and the manner in which we may overcome the problem of evil.

Such then are five fundamental special categories that shape theology. They respond to the questions, how do I experience God in my life? How do we experience it together? Where does such an experience come from? How do we judge it? How does it help us overcome our problem of evil?

Models

It is one thing to have basic categories. The reality they deal with pervades all cultures. It is another thing to express ourselves with models. These pertain to different cultures. Models are relative. For to speak of a model is not to speak immediately of a way of summing up reality, but more precisely, as a way of engaging in the exploration of it. Models are maps. They may or may not be true.[5]

At this point, it is worth indicating that the greatest confusion tends to come into theological expression here. As in the New Testament itself, so in all ages of theology, different schematic images (models) shape our expression of reality.

The role of models is quite modest. They shape the manner of our entry into the question. If you want to explore the atomic and infra-atomic world, you must have some schematic

14

image of what you are likely to find. It may or may not be a good description. But, at least, its limitations will be exposed, and you may be left with a more healthy respect for the complexity of the reality in question. I might think of atoms as little planets or solar systems. And, indeed, that type of image will get me so far. But then a new range of data demands that I complement my exploration with another type of map or model, a field of waves, or a field of energy, or a haze of all these things.

Now a similar situation obtains in theology. I may approach the mystery of the incarnation as God coming to man, or man progressively opening himself to God; I may use a more evolutionary image, God as the radical force of evolution expressing himself from within the process, so that the whole cosmos attains a new type of consciousness, has a new field of inter-action, a qualitatively new type of future.

Models are only tentatively expressive. They must be tested by the data. They shape our approach to reality along either legal, psychological, cosmic, personal, dynamic, static, communitarian lines — or any combination of these. They give an emphasis and an outlook. They are *expressive* models.[6]

However, there is another range of models that are more aptly called *experiential*. These deal with the way we understand the experience of ourselves, with others, in a world, before God, etc. We might feel ourselves to be the centre of the universe or the crown of creation. We might identify ourselves as a wayward and alienated individual or apprehend ourselves as a rung, higher or lower, on the ladder of cosmic evolution. We might feel our religious life to be an inner illumination, or the bond of community, an immersion in the development of the cosmos, a way to the future, or a force for the political transformation of society, as an affair of the heart or the highest business of the head.

Such experiential models shape our expressive models. I tend to speak of God the way I experience myself. Further, our expressive models tend to focus our experience and consequently our experiential models. If I speak of the cosmic Christ, I might well inspire people to attend to the cosmic dimensions of their own existence, and to appreciate it in a new way.

But models come and go. Some are successful. Some, are modish, the result of vogue. Others respond to a spontaneous, indefinable experience of our world, so that we are inclined to say, "this is the way in which I should explore the Mysteries of life."

Whatever the case, theological expression is shaped by them. And to the degree we realise this, a healthy relativity comes into theology. We come to a keener sense of exploration. Theology assumes a more modest and flexible proportion. It remains open to completion, the kind of completion that postmodern science is not slow to teach us about, since it learnt this kind of humility first.[7]

And so, with symbols and story, with categories and models, we have a brief schema on the expressions of theology. Such a schema, accepted, revised or rejected, can only bring clarity into the enterprise of plotting the ever surprising paths of the living God amongst us.

1. See the fine book, Mary Douglas, *Natural Symbols. Explorations in Cosmology* (Pantheon Books: New York, 1970).

2. See Harald Weinrich, "Narrative Theology", *Concilium* 5 (May, 1973), 46-56; Johann Baptist Metz, "A Short Apology for Narrative", *ibid.*, 84-98.

3. See John Flynn, M.S.C., Fairy Tales and Gospel Heroes", *Compass* (October, 1973), 3-9, commenting perceptively on some modern literature, especially Rosemary Haughton's *Tales from Eternity* (Allen and Unwin, London, 1973), and of course, the writings of Tolkien.

4. See Bernard Lonergan, *Method in Theology* (DLT: London, 1971), 281-288.

5. *Op.cit.*, 288-292.

6. Ewert Cousins, "Models and the Future of Theology", *Continuum* 7 (Winter-Spring, 1969), 78-92; I. Ramsey, *Models and Mystery* (London, 1964); J. McIntyre, *The Shape of Christology* (London, 1966); W. Austin, "Models, Mystery and Paradox in Ian Ramsey", *Journal for the Scientific Study of Religion VII* (1968), 41-55.

7. We have an excellent book in this whole area in Harold K. Schilling, *The New Consciousness in Science and Religion* (SCM: London, 1973).

2

The Gospel story

IN THE beginning was the Word . . . God, in the originality of his being, affirms all that he is, and all that we are, shall be, and could be. The Word is the affirmation of all life, express and complete . . . And the Word was made flesh, and dwelt amongst us . . . The affirmation of all that God is, and of all that might be, it uttered into our history. It is heard in the heart of each of us.

In the darkness, pain and limitation of human existence, Jesus stands forth as the affirmation of life. He is the affirmer and the affirmed. He is the Yes to all God's promises, and the Amen to all our prayers.

The Story of the Word

As expressed in his human existence, the Word has a history. Jesus is born, lives, suffers, dies, rises. As he enters into the heart and mind of believers, the Word becomes a story. As projected into the history of all men and women, in all times, in all cultures, the Word becomes a story told and retold. The occasions for such retellings are as frequent as the number of the life-stories of men and women who hope that their story is a good story. The Word becomes the way of telling our story, the way of accounting for how we belong together, from the beginning unto the end.

The Word becomes the story, the Gospel. He does not become first of all doctrine or dogma or theology. Each of these is only part of his story. And so, it is essential to note the narrative of how the Word lives amongst us and invites us to listen.

The contemporary world is marked by differing strands of experience conveying streams of thought, impulses of feeling, levels of experience, degrees of involvement, intuitions of reality. In all their astonishing variety, these mix, collide, merge and conflict. In such confusion, one temptation is to withdraw into a rigid dogmatism, in which everything is seen as finished and fixed. From this position, one has no story to tell, only a formulation of truth to be shouted in a vain attempt to get a hearing. Others can be excused for wondering if truth, which is the unrestricted fulfilment of the human mind, could be so small and so controlled. The other temptation is to become all-tolerant. We can easily become so open to such a variety of views and attitudes, that we can be challenged with the question of whether we wish to tell the truth at all? Is our openness an emptiness? We may not be a slave of the past; perhaps we are just victims of the present. Have we a story to tell?

The older categories crack and strain. The old wineskins swell dangerously with the ebullient new wine. The shout of a defensive dogmatism is as unacceptable as the bland reticence of the over-tolerant. We must begin to search for modes of expressions that truly enable minds to meet, but which invite us to live out of a definite past in the direction of a hopeful future. At this point, the simple, largely unnoticed expressiveness of the story comes quietly into its own.

Stories

The story is fundamental. It makes no pretensions. It tells; it does not theorize; it does not explain, expound, compare or bring together. It aims to be nothing but itself, for it knows no criteria outside itself. The story pervades all cultures and touches all peoples, whether it be the primitive myth of the ancients, the drama of Shakespeare, a Victorian novel, a contemporary allegory or modern Western on the screen. The story offers a memory, and thereby an invitation to share in an experience that happened "once upon a time", thence to be held as significant for all the times of our history.

In the beginning was the Word . . . and the Word became a story; and those who listen to it themselves become story-tellers, for the sake of all those who are concerned with the unfinished story of humanity.

Now it is possible for Christians to forget that they are essentially story-tellers. We can easily forget that the story is not finished, least of all with us! The story of humanity seems to grind to a halt when any one age takes itself too seriously. Life is frozen in the rigid present; we become too full of ourselves to tell other stories. It is possible, too, for theology to forget its purpose, which can only be to make the telling of the Gospel story more . . . telling. When theology seeks to make the Gospels more telling, it makes all human stories more tellable in the light of the simplicity and tenderness of the Gospel. If theology becomes some abstract lore, it loses itself in the wisdom of the world. It must then experience a universal inattentiveness, because, quite simply, it has no wonderful story to tell. It no longer tells or listens to its own story.

We never seem quite capable of coping with the most surprising story that has ever been told. As far as stories go, it is one with too much folly and too much love, surprisingly blended in God and ourselves: God's folly and human folly in the cross; God's love and human love in the totality of the gift of self that is demanded. For the story of the Gospel is the story of one more good man "who went about doing good". He spoke of a great crisis that had come into human affairs: we could be given life and light, if only we would prefer it over death and darkness. This man told God's story with the claim that he really knew it; he offered his story to human beings in a language of friendship and brotherhood that defied the seemingly necessary conventions of class, politics, religion and culture. But this kind of story is one of too much failure: his death was brought about by the very forces he most opposed, by the forces of "reality" and expediency that could not abide the possibility of there being a more beautiful story about life.

It is a story not only of too much failure, but of too much victory. It leads to surprising triumph. It offers a kind of hope which, along with being a joy that liberates man in the darkness of his life, is a continuing riddle for the human mind. He rose from the dead. The words of the story-tellers cannot say more. The old words exhaust themselves. They were not shaped to convey such a fullness of life. Yet his rising to new life is the point of the story. The resurrection makes the story of Jesus a good story, worth the telling from generation unto generation. As generations have come and gone, lived and died these two thousand years, this surprising story can lay a just claim to being "the greatest story ever told".

By being the story of Jesus, it is the story of everyman. Everyone can hear this story as his own. It is my story, yet not the way an autobiography is. I might try to tell my story and give myself a name in the hope that someone might listen, and think my story worth the telling. But here is the bankruptcy of the autobiography — I am simply not here to tell the whole story of my life, how it ended, and how it entered into the lives of others who come after.

Nor is the Gospel a simple biography. Perhaps someone will "write my life" if I am judged to have a life-story worth the telling. Then I depend on others for my real name. The judgment on who I am passes out of my hands into the hands of others. But the "other" has simply not experienced what I am from the inside; and he himself is merely a limited human being.

The Gospel story of *my* life is neither autobiography nor biography. It is something different. This difference lies in its being the story of God, of the God who knows me more than I have come to know myself. The Word indeed becomes a story for us, but only because it is the story of such a God. It begins as the biography of God in our world: the Word was made flesh . . . "the only Son who dwells nearest the Father's heart has made him known" (Jn 1, 18). God's story is told in his adventure into humanity, in his abiding concern for every human being, in love, failure and triumph. Such a story invites us to hear of God as the friend in our lives, as the one who truly knows what is in man, and in each of us. It evokes the hidden depths in all of us, for our story is revealed as part of his story.

Yet such a story is not really completely told if we leave it at this. If we continue to speak about God "in the third person", as in a story about him, the story of the Gospel has failed. We must be led to appreciate this story as the auto-biography of God. God is presented as telling his story to me: "I have loved you with an everlasting love. I have treasured your being as long as I have been God, and had my joy in it. I offer myself as a mystery of Love available in the telling of your story, so that no matter how you or anyone else will tell your story, you remain forever part of my story; you are part of the happy ending; you are meant to live happily ever after . . . with me!"

God's Story and Faith

This transition from hearing the biography of God to appreciating the autobiography of God is faith. We are caught up into God's own story as he tells it: how he is carried away, beside himself, in compassion for our humanness; how he empties himself to take the last place amongst us, rejected, vulnerable unto death, his glory concealed until he has com-pleted his pilgrimage into the darkness of the human heart, and found a burial in a human tomb. Only then is the secret of Life revealed, that Love is stronger than death. Such a Love means resurrection. Resurrection is the surprise of a life-time.

It is all this that makes the story of Jesus a good story full of surprising grace.

Yet an objection is raised with all the force of our being conditioned against it: our faith is more than a story. It is truth. It is doctrine. It is the formula, fixed and definite, time-less and complete. It is reality. It is a fact. And the fact is the reality, whereas the story is not . . . It is . . . only a story.

Is it? Certainly the story is not absolutely fixed because it is told and retold in all the conditions of life. It evokes a variety of responses and is open to all kinds of interpretations to the degree it draws each of us into itself. The story is not timeless since it exists only in time. It is about the time of living, of someone's life, told for the enjoyment of our time. Neither does the story have the stark unity of scientific fact, for it comprises so many unpredictable elements and so many "unnecessary" details: it has the unity of a dance as opposed to the unity of skeleton. Nor is the story controllable . . . how will someone else tell the story we have passed on to them? It escapes our ideas of beginning and end: it starts "once upon a time" and ends in "happiness ever after". It is not programmed. The computer cannot tell a story.

Granted all this, one might ask whether the story is a flight from the real? I think not. Take for example that type of story which could be quickly dismissed as nonsense, the fairy story. It is peopled by all kinds of imaginary characters, elves, goblins, talking animals, wicked witches, good fairies and little people of long ago who walk through enchanted forests, sail on magic streams and live in golden castles and the deepest caves of the mountains. Is it real?

The whole thing stops being real when it stops being a story. Take it apart and you stop the story. The microscope might see the tiniest structures of organic life, but it cannot see the blooming of a rose or the smile of a child. Life tends to elude our analysis. Science generalises and abstracts whilst our living is particular and dynamic. The story, however, has its own kind of authority because it does not remove us from the actual experience of living. It does something to us in the midst of life. As we hear the story, a new ingredient enters our lives, and invites us to participate in the fundamental adventure of living in a fresh way, as affected by what has happened to others.

The Reality of the Story

At this point, the reality of the fairy story suggests itself. It is a story almost not worth the telling, so exposed and seemingly fragile are the beauties and promises of life. Yet the fairy story does evoke a universal quality of life. It is preeminently the story of the triumph of the defenceless human values. The charming prince arrives in the nick of time. The good fairy recovers her power at the last moment. The joyful reunion takes place when all seemed lost. Apparent death was only a sleep brought about by an evil spell. The shrewd calculations of the witch or the ogre or the rich and evil man are dramatically overturned. The little people win out. The beauty of life is revealed as the truth of life. An escape? Yes, but an escape into the true, surprising, quality of life: we are not finished, least of all when all seems lost. We break out of the prison into the free air of an existence where sudden and surprising grace overtakes us in the midst of darkness and imprisonment.[1]

In contrast to life's magic, facts, which become the dull literalism of existence, can be a way of closing ourselves to the full promise of life. The factual analysis can be a way of forcing our universe into the manageable patterns of our working relationship to it, thus cutting a great mystery down to size. We control, dissect, exploit to manage reality in proportion to our needs. The story, especially the fairy story, has its reality only as an invitation . . . to be open to the real drama of life with all its light and darkness. Yet when the end is offered to us, it is in surprising grace.

The Gospel is the foundation of all such story-telling. The Good News legitimates this kind of flight of the imagination, and frees human fancy to conceive of reality in richer colours and greater dimensions and more surprising moments. For it is the story of the great catastrophe and the great grace, the latter arising out of the depths of the former. As a story, it explodes the pompous solemnity of so much of our living and invites us back to the dramatic and gracious mystery of true life. It is the story of the triumph of goodness, despite the terrible vulnerability of mankind's highest values.[2]

But there are sad stories. Indeed there are. Yet, in a true sense, a story loses its utter sadness when it is told: people listen, and share sympathetically a moment of life together, and in compassion, recognise the past as sad. In this moment, the sadness of the story is overcome: the total sadness is replaced by hopefulness, for the sad story has ended in its being heard in a wider circle of humanity, where before there was no one there to alleviate the tragedy. In such listening, humanity receives its "gift of tears"; and a determination is born to obliterate the sadness of the world, not by seeking to forget it, but by remembering it as part of the greater story of grace, joy and liberation. The sad story excites us to tell the whole story. And the whole story is the healing story. Some of the truth of life does hurt; but the whole truth does not. The whole truth is the story of the occurrence of amazing deliverance and surprising grace. It is the final good news. It is the Gospel.

There is a time for the telling of stories. If the cold light of dawn is the time for looking facts in the face, the evening is the time for letting stories into our lives. The work of the day is over. We are open to the larger dimensions of life. This is the time of tenderness, of communion, for gathering round the fire, for sharing the meal, and the merriment of wine. This becomes the moment of recollection, of recalling the past, since it is the recollection of ourslves on our way to an as yet unknown future. The story becomes the expression of our essential communion in the adventure of existence. We cannot refuse to listen, for there is a strange authority about a story. It is the narrative of grace in time. Perhaps in the morning we might ask whether it was true. Our only question in the evening can be, "how does it invite us to live?"

Of course, there is something vaguely ridiculous to spend time in writing about stories. The Word who became a story did not write at all — a reminder that no story can really be put onto a page or stuffed into a book. The home of the story is human sympathy, the union and reunion of humanity in a moment of leisure, in a moment of grace, when we turn to one another and ask, "what is your story?" . . . "what is the story we share?"

1. For the most comprehensive treatment, see J. Navone and T. Cooper, *Tellers of the Word* (Le Jacq: NY, 1981).
2. See J. R. R. Tolkien, *Tree and Leaf* (Unwin: London, 1964).

3

Experience and theology

WITH such a vast and elusive subject, modesty is the best policy. Nonetheless, given that our treatment is necessarily schematic, I will draw in broad strokes on a rather large canvas, modesty or not!

But it is a vast and elusive area. We all talk about experiences, and feel we must; this counteracts any understanding of theology as an abstract dogmatism or a higher logic spiralling off into irrelevance, or even a mountain of meticulous scholarship finally forgetful of its original purpose. There is no doubting the good intentions of anyone calling for a more experienced base and scope of theological thinking. The problem is how to get hold of all that significant experience. And whose experience?

The clinching arguments of the old (presumably wiser) was once, "speaking from experience". Now an appeal to experience is likely to be demanded of the more youthful who are impatient with the hallowed, plodding, abstract formulations of the "faith of our fathers".

How do we understand "experience"? Some see it as a great ocean in which we are immersed with its tides, currents and sudden undertows, with theological theory teaching us how to swim or navigate (depending on the degree of our immersion). Others see it as a fresh coat of paint to be applied to a solid old home — the better to highlight the sturdy and hospitable features of this traditional theological dwelling. Yet others seemingly understand theology as a pot-plant growing unobtrusively in one's study to be watered by "common experience", and nourished from time to time with a more specialised "indoor plant nutrient", an optional rather mysterious extra of "special experience" which one can easily overdo.

Whatever our metaphorical preferences, we can easily catalogue "rhetorics of experience". A few years ago, I isolated seven such rhetorics and four philosophical approaches, each with its own understanding of experience (*Compass,* Aug., 1975). So, with some awareness of the linguistic philosophical complexity of the issue, I offer this theological note.

1. *A General Systematic Approach*:

I think there is some merit in suggesting a general approach to the question of the inter-relationship of theology and experience. It could be put this way: theology is practical, critical, imaginative reflection on the experience of faith in its past, present and future dimensions. More subtly, theological experience lives from an evocation of the past quality of experience, the awareness of oneself experiencing it, and the consciousness of oneself caught up and committed to a new emerging kind of experience toward the future.

Perhaps it will be a little clearer if we reverse the past/present/future dimensions of experience in its relation to theology. Let us begin with:

Experience Moving toward the Future:

Pedagogically and, to my mind, methodologically, experience is most intrusive and challenging in theological reflection when it is an orientation toward the future. Theology is not merely an intellectual *product* of reflection but a *conduct* of life in the world. It is a way of freely involving oneself in the process of "man's making of man". Here lies the much analysed modern notion of praxis; for our theological thinking is doing something. It modifies and is affected by the interests and concerns of our action. This implies that theology comes out of and moves into a deep way of experiencing reality, as it is — or how we feel it should be. In our day it is obviously determined by all the negative experiences of dislocation, injustice and dehumanisation; and by hope, too, grounded in the presentiment of new graces being offered to our stricken and limited humanness, in terms of global community, peace, healthy secularity.

From this point of view, theology lives from an experience of involvement in the future; a conduct in the formation of what is coming to be — an experience of what is emerging.

Experience in the Present:

This experience of involvement and "conduct" lives from a more interior type of experience: the consciousness of oneself. This is constituted as authentic selfhood only as we recognise and promote the full unfolding of our consciousness on its various levels. Now there is nothing very mystifying about this for it means simply: I cannot give myself to the world's work unless I am critically open to the experience of being someone who senses, feels, imagines; who asks questions, forms ideas, makes judgments; who assumes moral responsibility; who, in and through all this, abandons himself to the Spirit of faith, hope and love working within. Indeed, if I am a Christian, I experience the presence of Christ as essentially the horizon of all my feeling, thinking, judging, acting and loving.

I am indicating here the pivotal point of our theological integration of experience: that appropriation of the experience of oneself as a self, a self that demands to be recognised, affirmed, respected, promoted in all its dynamic unfolding if I am to live an authentically human life "in good conscience". This experience of dynamic self-possession brings with it a demand to be open to the experience of meaning, of truth, of value, of mystery, of redemption. It is certainly a "present experience" but in the deepest sense of being an experience of self-presence, the presence of that many-levelled self involved in and interacting with, the world we share and form. (B. Lonergan, *Method in Theology,* p. 267 ff).

It is really the experience of a self summoned into the process of conversion of a self hearing the reverberations of the imperative to be open, to be attentive, to be honest, to be reasonable, to be self-creating and self-surrendering — to be, ultimately speaking, in love with what eye has not seen nor ear heard nor the heart conceived. It is this experience of self experiencing its summons to be totally "for Christ", in all the senses we have just listed, which is at the foundation of the project and conduct of theology.

Experience of the Past:

Now this brings us to that other dimension of experience, the past. For in recall, in research, in memory, the theologian experiences "their experience". This experience of the past enters into our experience of the present and future as shaping it with its resources of feeling, acting, believing, for the expression of our separate identities as Christian, Catholic, Orthodox, Protestant and so on. Paradoxically, the extraordinarily meticulous scholarship of modern Biblical Philology, exegesis, textual criticism can, in all its detailed array, obscure our sense of the data of the past as a record of experience, of "how they experienced" the irrevocably new thing that had happened. So I think we should be firm and clear on this simple point: before it gives us any particular genre or technical term or ethical principle of theology, the Bible presents us with a record of experience.

And if it is a record of experience, it is not surprising that the deep structure of this experience is narrative. The Gospel subsumes dozens of particular stories into the one narration of "how God so loved the world". Hidden in this is the biography, as it were, of the Chosen People with the great originative story of Exodus. More explicitly, it is the autobiography of a people and a community, of a "we" that came to identify the One God as "our God". More deeply, through all such narrative, we are being presented with a biography of God, creator of the world, liberator of Israel, who sends his Son "in these last days" (Heb 1, 2). And at the nub of such a narrative, is the autobiography of God, from the "I am who I am" of Exodus to the opening of the heavens, the descent of the dove and the voice from above, "Thou art my beloved Son: with thee I am well pleased! (Mk 1, 11).

Such a narrative of experience is related through many

rhetorics, the ways of making the original experience more telling. There is the rhetoric of fulfilment: the sense of how all things find their fulfilment in Christ, the Omega Point: "finally, in these last days" (Heb 1, 2). Then there is the rhetoric of participation: the new order of existence can be experienced only inasmuch as we who came after find a sacramental and mystical communion with the experience of Christ in his death and resurrection (Rm 6, 11). Thirdly, there is the rhetoric of cosmic extension: faith in Christ is overture to a universal experience of consistency and coherence. "He is before all things and all things hold together in him" (Col 1, 17). Other such rhetorics could be suggested.[2]

But the point at the moment is that the experience of the past is narrated in a variety of rhetorics to involve us in a "telling experience" in our present. It has been narrated in many ways by Paul and John and the Synoptics, by the great mystics, doctors and martyrs, by the reformers and the pastors of the tradition. Less obviously, the great councils are involved in a process of keeping the original narrative open and moving: they interrupt its easy flow to ensure that the whole remains a telling experience, or, better, an experience worth the telling. It would be interesting to take up the Council of Chalcedon in this way . . . but not here. So too, ritual and art; and last, and probably the least, theology, using all the resources of its many methods, works to establish the right mood, to get the original story a hearing in all the variety of cultures and successive epochs of history.

Underlying all this are different patterns of experience: the mystical, the intellectual, the esthetic, the prophetic. These give their own accent to the narration of what was going on in those days which has come forward to meet us in our own. Before we examine the past as a collection of texts or dogmatic data or moral persuasion or theological system, it comes to us as a fund of experience.

As such it enters our present to invite and inspire a retelling of its story in the first person: as the "they" now yield to the creative response of the "we", the story is retold to enkindle afresh its original Gospel in a wider world of new opportunities and more global awareness of the need of Good News.

So much, then, for a general statement of the experiential infrastructure of theology. The remaining question regards the variety of ways theological reflection can lay hold of this essential, many-levelled fund of experience. To this we now turn.

2. Three Models

Admittedly there are dozens of ways one could suggest of relating experience to theology. Here I will mention just three models for achieving this: the first is in terms of psychological interiority; the second looks to the social structure of shared religious experience; the third is concerned with the esthetically public and paradigmatic character of the classics of tradition.

1. Psychological Interiority: Lonergan's Notion of Religious Love:

Lonergan's notion of religious love is one way for theology to lay hold of religious experience in depth. He understands this dynamic state of being-in-love as the fulfilment of existential self-transcendence (*Method,* 101-8). It is at once a homecoming and a continuing pilgrimage for the self in this experience of self-surrender. The kind of loving he speaks of is a transcendent giftedness penetrating and directing every level of our existence. However, Lonergan locates it at the topmost level of the unfolding of selfhood, the point where the person commits himself to the meaning of all meaning and the worthwhileness of all value.

Now this being-in-love without restrictions of qualifications fulfils our conscious intentional striving. The capacity to be beyond ourselves in the exploration of meaning, to live beholden to truth, to be morally committed to values, to find some ultimate point of belonging and surrender becomes an actuality with this gift of religious loving. Though it is a conscious state in which judgments and decisions can occur, it is above all a consciousness of fulfilment of all basic human striving — a point of conversion to the ultimate. Though this can be broadened and deepened and enriched, it cannot be super-seded. It occupies the highest point of human development, the "apex animae", the peak of the soul.

In Lonergan's terminology, this state of transcendent loving "sublates" all the dynamics of self-transcendence. Our capacities to go beyond ourselves toward meaning, truth and values are now taken up into a new level of conscious living. Such a sublation preserves all the proper features of other levels of our conscious existence (intellectual, rational, moral . . .) but now carries them forward "to a fuller realisation in a richer context" (p. 241).

By referring to the work of F. Heiler, Lonergan goes on to suggest that his account of religious experience does in fact conform to the kind of experience witnessed to in the world's great religions.

Though this is all a very complex issue, our simple point must not be lost. For it is this: the experience of ultimate form of self-transcendence is at the heart of theological method. Unless theological reflection is animated by such a dynamic experience in oneself and others, theology can only be detached scholarship, or worse, a dogmatic ideology incapable of any collaboration with the globally human enterprise. If, however, it is grounded in such an experience, it can find a foundation for its categories, can give sense to its terms, direction to its practice and breadth to its dialogue. For it is experimentally grounded in what is consciously accessible to all good people who go beyond themselves for the sake of something more.

Through this kind of intentionality analysis, experience finds its place at the foundation of theology, especially the depth and breadth of mystical experience. A concrete example of this is W. Johnston's *The Inner Eye of Love* (Harper and Rowe, 1978).

Nonetheless, there is another model which, in the long run, may prove to be more publicly accessible:

2. The Social Structure of Religious Experience:

This is suggested by Clifford Geertz' description of religion as a sociologically given way of life. His descriptive definition of religion is well known:

"A system of symbols acts to establish powerful, pervasive and long-lasting moods and motivations in man by formulating conceptions of a general order of existence; and clothing these conceptions with such an aura of factuality that the moods and motivations seem uniquely realistic" (*Anthropological Approaches to the Study of Religion,* ed., M. Banton, Tavistock, 1963). His four points are useful for establishing a socially given field of experience in which one can earth the theological process of reflection: a system of symbols; moods and motivations emanating from such a symbolic system, the resultant conception of a general order of existence; the aura of factuality and realism. A word on each of these:

(1) *A system of symbols*: Just how you work the extraordinary range of symbols into a system might be a problem, but basic symbols, each one evocative of a type of experience of God, self and the world, certainly abound: The Incarnation, Cross and Resurrection, The Trinity, Mary, the Communion of Saints, the Sacraments . . .

(2) *Moods and Motivations*: Thanksgiving, the sense of the utterly New, hope, repentance, urgency, contemplative wonder . . . These are moods from which Christian tradition lives; and the motivations? "If God has so loved us, we ought also love one another". All the variety of motivation resulting from the revelation of God's unqualified love in Christ are easily accessible in the biblical documents and wealth of spiritual writings deriving from them.

(3) *The Order of Existence*: This is clearly built around the central redemptive fact of Christ . . . "nothing in all creation can separate us from the love of God in Christ Jesus" (Rm 8, 39). "He is before all things and in him all things hold together" (Col 1, 17).

(4) *The Aura of Factuality*: The Catholic sense of the real sacramental presence of Christ would be important here, the classic Protestant notion of Justification, the

Orthodox experience of Spirit and Ikon; and basic to all this, "If Christ be not risen from the dead, then your faith is futile", etc. of 1 Cor 15, 12-19.

These four points could be worked up into a very valuable resource for a more experimental type of theological reflection. Whether or not such a form of experience establishes sympathetic vibrations in the thinker, inviting him to join such an experiment of faith, is a critical question. If it does not — well, that may be sad, but at least it is honest. If it does, then there is work to be done! We will have to go on to own the given experience critically, creatively, practically, from the inside, to let the whole thing speak, catch us up and carry us on. Theology will be earthed not only in the heart but in the living communication of a given historical community. This brings us to the third model.

3. The Aesthetic Paradigm: Tracy's Notion of The Classic:

David Tracy expounds his notion of the classic in his formidable *The Analogical Imagination* (Crossroads, 1981). Given the complexity of the issue, I think it would be pardonable to make these five simple points:

1. Tracy presents his notion of the classic to counteract the modern tendency to reduce (faith and art) to a private area of subjectivity divorced from the public domain of reality. By appealing to the classics of the tradition, theology can regain a legitimate and indeed quite necessary public voice — if it is to be true to the universal meaning of the Gospel.

2. The appeal to the classic has an edge to it, too: for in "going public" via the classics, theology has a way of challenging the monodimensional basically uncritical technocratic features of contemporary culture with something that is intrinsically authoritative and paradigmatic as an expression of experience. The classic challenges and refreshes the tight narrow scope of modern experience with its inexhaustible "plus".

3. Classics are undeniably present in every culture. Tracy

understands the term to extend to texts, images, symbols, events, rituals and even persons. But his point is that through them "we have a disclosure of reality we cannot but name truth" (p. 108). The recognition of the authentically human classics provoke "surprises, challenges, shocks and eventually transforms us" (*ibid*). The classic draws us out of our routine perceptions of reality to a vision of the ultimately human . . . and Christian.

4. The classics achieve their effect by drawing us out of our critical controlling approaches into a play of conversation in which we surrender to the authority of the classic, let ourselves be interpreted by it — in contrast to controlling it from some critical vantage point. We let the classic lead us in allowing it to have its own given authority.

5. Though this notion of classic may seem hopelessly broad, I think it not unlikely that we could all agree on some classics, and that, in any theological context, a start can be made. We can re-read and let ourselves be interpreted by the great psalms, by Paul to the Romans, by each of the Gospels, by Augustine's *Confessions,* by Pascal's *Pensees,* Teilhard's *Le Milieu Divin,* by Raphael's Madonnas, Beethoven's Ninth Symphony . . . the Cathedral of Chartres!

Theology becomes a kind of critical art in establishing the right time, space and mood so that the classics of past and present are free to take over and speak their enduring and inexhaustible message. As I say, a few doctoral theses will be needed before we can evaluate Tracy's work in any adequate way. In the meantime, we have sufficient classics to keep us going for a hundred lifetimes . . . sufficient to underline the fact that Tracy's point is a point well made in a timely way.

For the moment, I am simply emphasising that theology can refresh itself immeasurably by constructing itself round the paradigm experiences of human truth as they come to expression in the classics. For the classic evokes for us both the wonder of existence and the meaning and range of self-transcendence. It is inherently a carrier of the symbols, moods, motivations and sense of reality that hold a given community together.

Such then are three models for relating experience to theology. Lonergan's is "from the inside-out"; Geertz's "from the outside-in"; Tracy's from the "here-and-now yet inexhaustibly beyond". Theology will tend to give prominence to now one, now another; but they are not mutually exclusive. Taken singly or together they open the way to a more experientially grounded way of doing theology.

1. See Moira Creede, *Logos and Lord. A Study of the Cosmic Christology of Joseph Sittler* (Louvain: 1977). Unpublished.

4

Theology and the mystery of God

RECENTLY a woman taking instructions asked, "Why aren't you Christians willing to speak about God?" The question was very significant since she had come from a Marxist and atheistic background. She had found that she could get all sorts of religious information. Apparently, much of it had appeared to be beside the point. For her, the real issue was God. And on that basic issue she considered that we had little to say. I must confess that my effort to answer her question did rather limp. But it did make me think. And the following observations are influenced by what I thought on that occasion.

Religion can get lost in endless arguments and observations on organisational and ethical issues. It then becomes a sophisticated distraction from the fundamental meaning of existence. Who amongst us, with all our re-thinking, renewal, restructuring and new orientations, is the true radical? Is theology a more or less endless commentary on matters of ecclesiastical policy or concern? Is it a scholarly reinterpretation of the sources of tradition? Is it an analysis of the more positive values of human culture as a preparation for preaching? All these things, of course. But there is something fundamental. In the face of life's absurdities, the main task of theology is to lead back to the one, simple, inexhaustible mystery. No matter what human progress or decline, no matter what is the prevailing philosophy or the quality of cultural achievement, theology must speak of God. This is its weakness and its strength. By definition, it can never adequately do this. But as it presses on to this goal, it gives expression to ultimate meaning wherein all the complexities of human existence have their resolution.

In recent times, theology has been understood more as an agency in the development of doctrine. More and more aspects of God and his revelation to man are deduced and discussed. But more fundamental than this extensive developing function of theology, is its intensive, simplifying task, as it concentrates the human mind on the meaning of God and interprets all human existence in the light of the One Mystery. Karl Rahner, more than any other modern theologian, has represented this point of view.[1]

God Is

The affirmation, "God is" stands, in faith, as the simple radiant truth of life. It is the more universal statement of "Alleluia, Christ is risen!" For if it is true that God really is, the universe is full of wonder and fascination. It is a hopeful place: there can never be an adequate inventory of resources, for nothing is finished, and nothing can be excluded as impossible or too hopeful. We remythologise and demythologise, exegete, reflect, expound, systematise, so treating of all the particular material of theology. If all this effort leads in the end to a loss of the original Mystery from which all this concern proceeds, a terrible sterility results. There are barren wastelands of theology to prove it. Theology, instead of elucidating and simplifying the mystery of faith, can trivialise and desiccate it.

Our contemporary, incredible naivete which reduces everything to scientific statements, must always be taken into account. The caricature of the "scientific mind" cannot see the real bearing of symbolic, personal and evocative statements and expressions. Not only is theology as talk about God declared to be impossible but scientific methodology is also impoverished. A kind of Catch 22 process emerges: you cannot speak about God unless you do so scientifically. But to speak scientifically rules out the possibility of speaking about God, since scientific method is limited to what can be the subject of experiment through measurement, weighing, testing. And it is true that the Living God is simply not so tractable. The real problem is that, in attempting to be intelligent about reality through scientific method, we neglect to be *very* intelligent about it (as T. S. Eliot suggests): we do not use our intelligence to see that reality is infinitely more inexhaustible, more delicate, complex, more intimate and wonderful, finally more simple, than a text book or a computer or a laboratory can admit. Science brings certain types of precision into human life. But that is not to say that living human beings need to wait for science to tell them everything about reality. Otherwise, no one would ever fall in love . . . and no one would ever surrender to the ways of the Living God.

Theology assists faith to give expression to its thrust in the direction of the ultimate reality. The objectivity of theological reflection is not in a contemplation of the human condition but in the adoration of the Divine Mystery. If theology should suffer from a forgetfulness of God in some way, and so lose its objectivity, faith cannot but appear as a personal or communal therapy for dealing with the big, threatening world. And if the theologian succeeds in not giving offence, it is because he is very flexibly legitimating a harmless fantasy.

God, Theology, Culture

To me it seems that the basically theological questions are still theological. It is true that in recent decades, theological thinkers have been explicitating the anthropological structure of theology ("for us men and our salvation"). Theology is not addressed to God. It is a word of hope for human beings, and takes shape in human minds. How theological can theology afford to be?

In modern culture, religion has been identified very explicitly as the enemy of human development. Marx saw "God" as the basic symbol of an economic system that pacified and exploited the poor. Freud saw "God" as the neurotic projection of the father-image which, in turn, repressed the energies of true human development. Nietzsche welcomed the death of the old god who had destroyed so much of genuine humanity, the one in whose name all the splendid powers of man were turned into vices, and all the pitiful features of human existence were exalted to the status of virtue. Such a god was the ancient enemy of true humanity. Sartre, with all the resources of Gallic literary elegance, carried this movement to its conclusion: no one can enjoy his human freedom unless he rid himself once and for all of the idea of God. Along with these philosophical positions went the pervasive ideology of the positivism of nineteenth century France. The positivist, supremely confident that the new age of science had arrived for the liberation of man, saw faith in God at best as a survival from the mythological or theological age that had preceded the modern era.[2] God was an unwarranted hypothesis. The phenomenon of religion would be studied in a detached and uninvolved manner by the new sciences of comparative religion, sociology, psychology and anthropology.

In such a cultural situation, theology feels compelled to establish its humanistic credentials. Simply, it must show its concern for humanity; and, more profoundly, it must bring out the real character of the salvation to be found in God. This does not mean that the Ultimate Mystery of Love and freedom that has communicated itself through Christ, is to be collapsed into some easily recognisable existential meaning. The Living God is more than part of the "quality of life". Just as great art and great love do not fit into any ordinary categories, neither does great Grace. God offers a kind of living and demands a kind of dying that are beyond our easy expectations. For his presence is a resurrection and a crucifixion for the sake of a life of freedom and, indeed, of joy, the dimensions of which are a surprise to the human spirit. "Eye hath not seen nor ear heard, neither has it entered into the heart of man . . ." (1 Cor 2,9).

Theology invites our human existence to an ecstasy and a service which goes beyond the given human horizon. In speaking of God, it speaks of the goal and direction of the self-transcendence demanded of us for the sake of "life to the full". An ultimate sterility for theology would result if it became the bland legitimation of a spiritual narcissism. In place of articulating the meaning of following Christ in the doing of the Father's will for the sake of the reign of justice and peace, it can busy itself with a kind of soul culture or encourage some precious individual spirituality or become fixated on some inverted contemplative experience or engage dramatically in a cheap rhetoric of social revolution. If theology forgets its fundamental concentration on God, it too easily aids a sterile inversion. Barren subjectivism replaces the outreach of faith into Mystery.

The easy utopian humanism of last century has now yielded to a far more tentative and dubious state of mind. Disillusionment and despair are not unknown in our experience of world wars, the insanity of the arms race, well nigh global catastrophes of starvation and malnutrition, fierce local conflicts, political corruption and the mass greed of unjust economic systems. Theology has the opportunity to become the language of the final and absolute hope that is being offered to a splintered and hesitant humanity. Such a language of hope is possible only if our central doctrinal and ethical questions are located in the light of the mystery of God. Learned debates about the formation of the Gospels, the psychology of Christ, the nature of the resurrection, structures of the Church, the reform of the liturgy, the nature of Christian moral imperatives can seemingly be conducted without explicit reference to the Mystery from which they derived. Little wonder that such intense theological debates bring forth nothing but a yawn from what we fondly imagined to be the attentive secular world. Theology does not seem in such situations to add anything decisive to human reflection.

But the great issues remain: control of the earth's resources, distribution of the world's wealth, the preservation of a natural ecology, the quality of truly human environment, the challenge of the world population, right to life and racial conflicts, nuclear warfare and world peace. Unless there is a radical and persistent effort to lead all these issues back to faith as surrender to the Mystery of God, what can theology offer? Nothing but a timid and belated restatement of what, to other disciplines, had been long regarded as obvious.

God as Mystery

I do not mean that theology must give up the effort to speak intelligibly to the contemporary world. A cloying pious manner of speaking might not serve any purpose. Nonetheless, there comes a time when any worldly reality if it is to be appreciated for what it is, must be apprehended as "quid Dei", something *of God*. All worldly realities and events, even as they stand forth in their originality and independence, invite us back into the incomprehensible and inexhaustible Mystery. "Reductio in mysterium". Doctrine develops, but faith also simplifies. Doctrine extends as more features of God's revelation are recognised, depthed and communicated. Faith grows in concentration as more ages of the Church, more experiences of culture, more events of the world, are brought into the light of the one, luminous simple Mystery, "in which we live and move and have our being". So it is the main task of theology to bring the language of transcendence and final hope into the many languages of humanity. To stick to this purpose, great concentration is required, and, it would seem, an unusual degree of freedom from the compulsion to be popular. The final irony (and sterility) occurs when theology degenerates, in the midst of an agnostic culture, into a journalistic exchange over ecclesiastical policies; or into an enthusiastic reissue of "the findings of modern science". Neither of these options are of much interest to the really thoughtful people of our time. If faith and theology are to be ruled out of court by "the modern mind", we may as well suffer this for the right reason: that we spoke too much and too clearly of the One Mystery through which alone life is given to us.

Briefly, theology must pursue its own objectivity by concentrating on the ultimate meaning. It must be the language of Mystery. It must excite adoration. For only the sense of God as infinite and incomprehensible gives the words of theology a true value. How can theology presume to elucidate any of the Mystery of God or our humanity unless it has first entered into that intense darkness surrounding human existence? There words run out and ideas point beyond themselves. Such a darkness makes us appreciative of the light. How can theology be the "word about God" unless it is first familiar with the silence that surrounds the divine Mystery? For the most obvious thing about God is his silence. If theology can cherish its limited words in the atmosphere of such a silence, it may escape being religious noise, another type of learned chatter. Instead of being our reflective "word about God", theology can easily become words about words about God. The original experience is lost; the fundamental aim is forgotten: theological reflection becomes thrice removed from the edges and limits of human experience from which and to which it is meant to speak.

II

In this second section of this reflection, I will offer just four points:

(a) Contemplative leisure
(b) The unsettling edge of experience
(c) In the Spirit
(d) The God of Jesus

(a) Contemplative Leisure

It is not enough for theology to join in the exposure of current humanistic myths about man's self-sufficiency. There are practical problems. One of these is the preoccupied character of modern urban existence. There is the unremitting pressure of "future shock" and the tensions of "choice overload". Persistent self-advertising consumerism offers its blandishments and its threats. The pace and pressure of life induce a fatigue that is increasingly severe. Through the media all the anxieties and catastrophes of the world are brought into our own homes. The competitive spirit and the standards of professionalism urge us to greater effort and higher qualification. Often a nameless depression and sense of frustration all but undermine the genuine advances of what we have come to call "the Welfare State".

Is it, then, an exaggeration to ask whether anyone has the necessary leisure to experience the ultimate questions in an explicit way? I do not think so: the big questions take time, perhaps a whole lifetime to formulate in personal terms: what does it all mean? Is it worthwhile? Why? To whom am I finally responsible? How do we human beings belong to one another in the end? Is there a love stronger than death? Is there a healing Grace greater than all our familiar human evils?

The first move of theology is to stimulate such great questions in human consciousness, even to demand an adequate formulation of them. The Gospel, after all, is an answer to a question. If culture tends to cut us off from our great questions and genuine longings, how does theology cope with such a situation?

First, the precise problem must be identified. And here I think we can go further. There is not only the obscuring of the great questions (darkening of the intellect) but a diminished sense of freedom (weakening of the will). Our basic self-determination is trivialised and distracted by the sheer multiplicity of the comparatively insignificant choices and adaptations we must make. Our sense of responsibility is taken up, as it were, with comparisons and selections, preferences dealing with degrees of adaptation to the way of life which conditions us. In the sheer abundance of consumer items that compete for my attention and resources, in the very number of practical possibilities which are open in my life, with all the planning, adaptations and adjustments I must make, how deep is my freedom? With a sense of being spread so thin over the surface of life, what kind of decisions have I implicitly made? With my conscious time so used up, there is a profound sense in which I lack "free time".

And so, there is something of a problem when we exalt the notion of human liberty. How many modern men and women ever commit themselves to anything? Could it be that the style of modern life tends to make deep decision-making rather unlikely? Could it be that many do not believe in God because they believe in nothing? . . . or because they believe in everything, and hence see no special value in religious belief? I think we can experiment with the generalisation that modern urbanised humanity finds it difficult to give itself to anything. Fidelity is a problem. In the modern high-rise, a pet poodle poses fewer problems than a child.

In the face of such a "darkening of the intellect" and "weakening of the will," theology must learn a method of dramatising the ultimate questions.[3] Theologians must learn from the prophets "who are raised up against" the situation. Who might they be? Little contemplative groups, forgotten servants of the destitute and aged, educators truly committed to their students beyond prestige and exam results, professionals who value human beings, honest politicians. . . .

In the light of such a testimony, theology can assist the radical process of "calling into question" the culture, the style of life, the set of answers we have settled for. The meaning of God can be liberating truth only to those who are seeking the truth with ruthless honesty. And God can be a saving reality only to those who wish to give themselves totally to what is worthwhile.

The task of theology which we have here described as that of stimulating the ultimate type of question, is further illumined by this next point:

(b) The Unsettling Edge of Experience

Despite the bias that modern life shows against asking the ultimate question, human life goes on, with all its great moments, its joys, suffering and death. Theology not only stimulates questions but tries to put words on the answers that we implicitly find. That fascination with "Something or Someone" calling us to search for deeper values and a more honest service of our neighbour, so many types of new awareness and compassion, instruct theology on the manner in which it can speak of God. What is the "Holy Spirit" that lifts so many beyond individual concerns? What is the origin of the impulse to be more compassionate? Why do we maintain hope in the face of failure and death? Granting that evil is a problem, what of the mystery of so much love?

Theology points to the irreducible "plus" or "further"

in all profoundly human experiences. I say "irreducible" because such human depths resist adequate understanding unless we follow them through to a sense of the ultimate in worth and meaning. The sense of one-ness of the universe, the call to responsibility for oneself and others, wonderment at existence itself, the mysterious character of all forms of love, are some typical instances of the experiences that demand further understanding.

Perhaps one of the most accessible experiences in our time is that of dialogue. Genuine human meeting and communication can take place only through a shared experience of truth. If truth, accepted in all its unpredictable and limitless reality, is not the norm of meeting, dialogue is impossible. The persons involved are forced further apart. Barricaded against each other, mutual manipulation is the only possible relationship.

On the other hand, if truth is experienced as the zone of shared responsibility, both the foundation and direction of a common development are possessed. We experience ourselves and the other not as possessing the truth, owning it and using it for some limited purpose, but each as possessed and judged by it. This is an approach that Gandhi deeply appreciated: God is Truth, the Truth of all truths, and, as such, is possessed by no one, but still enables all to meet. Co-existence and co-humanity become possible. God is understood less as a transcendent Lord of all, more as the Go-Between God, the Only One in which a fractured human race can find a meeting . . . and healing.

Here we have simply referred to the task that theology has. It must give content to religious concepts. The more it grows in the skill of identifying the profundities of human experience, the more real will it make its God-talk.[4] Let me stress the further problem does remain: how do modern human beings come by the powers of recollection to identify, appreciate and reflect on such experiences? It might be that for most of us today the presence of God will come home to us in a rather uncomfortable manner. I would suggest a deep restlessness and an Ecclesiastes-like disillusionment with our modern way of life, (vanity of vanities . . .) as we see the gleaming, affluent, self-promoting modern way of life as so much triviality, the keen experience that our age is being judged, that some last chance is being offered to us to work for peace and justice. This type of recollection is giving us a more real idea of God than placid metaphysical contemplation. And, of course, the more our orientation to the ultimate is repressed and treated as some kind of taboo that cannot be discussed or clarified, the more inarticulate, pervasive and unsettling will be the feeling of crisis and emptiness. But, we are assured that God is greater than our hearts (1 Jn 3,20). We can presume that there will be unaccountable experiences of joy and hope also: ". . . that all shall be well, and all manner of being shall be well . . ."

Whatever the case, theology cannot prescribe what human beings will experience. It can only be attentive to what is really happening and offer its resources to clarify and identify the Mystery that is implied.

(c) In the Spirit

We have travelled a quick path from question to experience. Now we pass from experience to Spirit: the question hinted at in the depth of our experience. Our experience throws light on the reality of the Spirit.

From many points of view, it is clear that we must take far more seriously the essential role of the Spirit in our approach to God. He is the great gift that is given in the New Covenant; and Pentecost is an essential mystery in the meaning of the Church: the Holy Spirit continues to be given. God, in the New Testament experience of grace, is not to be considered as somehow outside or above our existence. He is, as Love, on the inside, as it were, transforming our hearts, and spiritually enabling us to taste, see and hear the reality of God. The indwelling Spirit gives communion in the Mystery of God and makes us intimates with the Father. (Rm 5,5).

Without this appreciation of the gift of the Spirit as a dynamic presence within human experiences, it is possible to overemphasise the "Supreme Father" notion of God. The Christian approaches God as Father only in and through the

46

Spirit communicated to us through Christ. Only through the Spirit of Love do we have that particular and personal knowledge of what *Father* means in the mystery of the Godhead.

In the same way, we can pretend to too much clarity (of a philosophical type) when we understand our knowledge of the Incarnate Word as the revelation of God. Without the Spirit, without that loving, unitive participation in the very being of Christ that the Spirit gives (as typified in the Eucharist), Christ cannot be truly known. He may appear as an historical religious founder, a moral leader, a wonder worker and so forth. However, it is only through the Spirit do we have that penetrating and unitive knowledge of Jesus as Lord, and appreciate his abiding presence in the Church.[5]

That the Spirit, and only the Spirit, was the medium of new living relationships with God and Christ was an obvious fact for the early Church.[6] We can question how the fundamental character of the presence and activity of the Spirit was obscured. One possible explanation has, in fact, little to do with theology at all, for it deals more with a cultural issue. Western civilisation has been dominated by an experience of reality which is called "paternal". The accent has been on the particular, the logical, the rational, the dutiful, the structured. Man is understood to "grow up", to break away from dependence of all kinds, to stand up as an individual, distinct and rational. To the degree that paternal experience of reality was stressed (and there is no denying that it did produce an impressive civilisation), the correlative maternal experience of being was diminished. This maternal experience regarded immersion in being as primary in comparison with ordered distinct individuality of the paternal experience. With immersion in being, there comes a yielding in confidence to the inherent dynamism and nurturing power of being, a reliance on reality to bring us forth and bear us on. It is this "immersed" or more technically, "participatory" character of our existence that was downplayed in the cultural development that has been the matrix of our theological thinking.[7]

The result was a one-sided experience of reality. This, in turn, highlighted the transcendent character of the Divine Paternity, a notion not unaffected by all types of human projections, fear, hunger for power, rationalism, etc. It seems to be a fair generalisation that today we are recovering the other dimension of experience, for now the accent is so often on the cosmic, mystical, supra-rational, immanent feminine range of values. This situation will be an opportunity for theology to elaborate a far more satisfactory theology of the Spirit. By so doing, God will appear less as the sovereign reality demanding our obedience from above, more as a nurturing, enabling presence within, inspiring the human person to go beyond himself in self-surrender and service.

Theology, then, cannot speak unless it appeals to the fundamental questions that open humanity to the meaning of God. But fundamental questions occur only as a reflection on experience. For that reason we have referred to the "unsettling edge of experience". But the reason why experience is of such a type can be found only in the gift of the Holy Spirit to our humanity. If human beings reach out for completion, it is because they are marked by the Spirit. For he is Love within the One Mystery of Life, the ecstasy of God for God, Unity achieved and consummated. But he is the Spirit of Christ, and so this brings us to our last point.

(d) The God of Jesus

I make these remarks with brevity. But the point is simple. The Spirit leads us to Jesus as the incarnate expression of God. Precisely here I would frame this question: has theology, especially systematic theology, taken as seriously as it should, the surprising character of the God that Jesus represents? I do not think it an exaggeration when it is suggested that theology has often smuggled the speculative ideas of pagan philosophy into its treatment of the God of Jesus. The heavy accent on the Unity, Immutability, Impassibility, absolutely transcendent nature of God has often all but obscured the surprises of revelation! Can it be true that God is the One who refuses to be anything else but Love? That his power operates under the guise of such particularity and weakness? That he is so given over to the world in compassion? Can

48

the cross really be a revelation of the extent of God's relationship to mankind?

The above are just some of the questions that are still asked with profit. It seems we tend to style God's relationship to the world of human beings in very metaphysical terms. Only with enormous flexibility and proportion can they begin to respect the earthy actuality of tears and blood, loud cries, torture and death that characterised the Emmanuel.

I must be content with that brief remark. The God of Jesus is always a surprise to our preconceptions. The Spirit leads us to involvement in Mystery, an invitation and an impulse hidden in all our deep experiences and ultimate questions.

To conclude: in the first part of this article, I stressed in a number of ways, the *theological* character of theology: it is, first and foremost, the language of Mystery. In the second part, four general remarks were made. A Conclusion? Only this: when theology remembers God, it becomes a great intellectual adventure. Its words are never adequate, but its subject is inexhaustible and fascinating.

1. See, for example, "Reflections on Methodology in Theology", *Theological Investigations II,* London, DLT, 1974, pp. 84-101. Also, my "Is Lonergan's *Method* adequate to Christian Mystery?", The *Thomist* XXXIX (1975) 437-470.

2. Very useful still is H. de Lubac, *The Drama of Atheist Humanism,* London, S&W, 1949.

3. A good example would be Michael Novak, "The Unawareness of God", in *The God Experience,* New York, Newman, 1971, pp. 6-29.

4. For a very useful treatment of this question, see Charles Meyer, *The Touch of God,* New York, Alba House, 1971.

5. I am thinking of the kind of theological reflection that I Cor 2, 10-16 provokes.

6. Especially I Cor 12, 1-11.

7. See Heribert Muehlen, "The Person of the Holy Spirit", in *The Holy Spirit and Power, The Catholic Charismatic Renewal,* ed. Kilian McDonnel, OSB, NY, Doubleday, 1975, pp. 11-32. He refers to the Work of Franz K. Mayer.

5

The trinitarian mystery of God

AT SOME moment in the development of one's theology, the mystery of the Trinity becomes either an intense and pervasive fascination or a completely irrelevant super-structure, — of, at best, antiquarian interest. St. Augustine, writing his *de Trinitate* over those sixteen years (400-416) "beginning them as a young man and finishing them as an old man", witnesses to the fascination: ". . . for nowhere else is the error more dangerous, the search more laborious and the results more rewarding". Kant represents the opposite view, shared not only by Liberal Protestantism, but by many a frustrated student of theology: "Absolutely nothing worthwhile for the practical life can be made out of the doctrine of the Trinity, even when one believes it is understood adequately, — and even less when one perceives that it exceeds our concepts".[1] It is always with a certain puzzlement that I have witnessed this polarisation; the reasons for it are, I suppose, many, — locked away in the usually hidden ways we experience faith and its challenge.

Today certainly there is an extraordinary creativity in trinitarian theology, making it all but impossible to keep up with the literature. There is Barth's magisterial retrieval of trinitarian doctrine in his *Church Dogmatics*. Moltmann's linking of the Trinity to the mystery of the Cross has been a great and dramatic achievement. Rahner's untiring identification of the immanent Trinity with the economic Trinity has made it much more appreciated as a "mystery of salvation". Muhlen has highlighted the dynamic communal aspects of the meaning of the tri-personal God, with his "I" of the Father, "Thou" of the son and "We" of the Holy Spirit. Lonergan has transposed the classical psychological analogy into a more modern intentionality analysis. Panikkar has offered a trinitarian interpretation of the great world religions. Duquoc has given us a psychological account of trinitarian symbolism . . . and on it goes.

Development abounds. In so many ways, the Trinity has moved, as a theological topic, to the foundations of theology. For it determines our basic standpoint and outlook: through its range of reference, theology has the opportunity to correlate its central concerns, God, Christ, human existence and the Church: it remains the Mystery to which all other "mysteries" point, the revelation from which all other divine communications derive. All our modern studies must necessarily re-evaluate the old questions: how is such a mystery manifest in the Bible? What is the significance of the great conciliar definitions of Nicaea and Constantinople? What formerly seemed to lead to cut and dried answers in these areas is now revealed as data of extraordinary complexity: neither the old answers nor the old questions seem quite to fit the case.

Let me say a word, then, about the manner in which the scriptural data can be considered. As regards the biblical witness to the Mystery of the Trinity, we come very quickly to a dead end if we try to "prove the Trinity from Scripture". The basic components of trinitarian doctrinal language are simply not to be found in the Bible: person, nature, relationship and so forth. What we do have in the scriptural data is a *foundation* for an ever deeper type of trinitarian reflection. But this depends on our ability to see the biblical data as primarily disclosing the experience of New Testament faith with, in some instances, only the beginnings of a conceptual account of its meaning. I will refer very briefly to three points related to this living experience of God in the original communities.

(a) First of all, there is the experience of the Church. It is always problematical to talk about experiences as though it were an electric current flowing from one age to another. All that, in fact, does remain when we look back two thousand years is, on the one hand, our own present experience with its origins in the past; and, on the other, the verbal or symbolic expressions of what was going on "in those days". Despite an obvious caution such as this, we need not be completely agnostic; for these expressions of the past, especially in the present case, the New Testament writings, do disclose a very decisive way of being in the world. They emerge out of an orientation to action, a quality of feeling, definite types of rhetorical expression — in short a way of facing and trans-forming the world of that time . . . in the obvious hope that what happened "in those days", in those who acted and thought and felt and lived in that now vanished form, might have decisive meaning for such as ourselves, these centuries later. The more refined our phenomenological techniques in exploring past consciousness, the more accessible this past experience might be.

Now trinitarian theology will be concerned with what we are perhaps calling too hurriedly, "the trinitarian way of being and acting in the world", disclosed in the expressions that come down to us from those early communities. This is not as far-fetched as we might be tempted to think. Whatever about the variety in the ways of expressing what was going on in the great happening of Christ, three vivid, definite impressions come through. The first that of "Spirit": there is a sense of corporately conscious involvement in a new level of life manifesting itself in a special intimacy of communion and an exhilarating strong sense of mission. Men and women communicate within a vital new medium which gifts them with fresh confident energies: "To each is given a manifesta-tion of the Spirit for the common good" (1 Cor 12, 7). They share this common "breath of fresh air" which in some immediate way is the atmosphere in which their new being in Christ can grow to its full significance. For this we look especially to the Acts of the Apostles and 1 Corinthians for our primary documentation.

The second vivid impression emerging from this original experience is that of being addressed by the Son in "these last days" (Hb 1,1f). The "many and various ways in which God spoke to our fathers" has reached a point of culmination: and such a culmination breaks out of all the categories that are available to interpret it, for God is manifest in an unheard of, new way. The shock of crucifixion and the surprise of resurrection leave the old categories, son of God, son of man, messiah, servant, Lord stretched to the limit: ". . . no one knows the Son except the Father . . ." (11,27). The unheard of Word has been spoken: the radically and inexpressibly new is amongst us.

The third vivid impression is to my mind the most difficult to express in a way that does justice to its freshness and the sense of liberation it conveys. Very simply put, in the Spirit of the Son, Christians now "know the Father". In the intimacy of love they invoke him as "Abba" (Rom 5,5; Gal 4,6). The ultimate, still dwelling paradoxically in "inaccessible light" (1 Tim 6, 16) has irreversibly revealed itself as mercy, as "Love", inviting Christians to a familiarity with the divine that nothing in all creation can sever or impede (Rom 8,37ff). God's dreaded ambiguities now yield to a liberated simplicity of faith and surrender: " . . . to have seen me is to have seen the Father" (Jn 14,9).

These three "vivid impressions", deriving as they do from the experience of the early Church, serve as fundamental orientations for theology. But at the heart of such experience is another pattern of experience, that of Jesus himself. Despite all the hermeneutical complexities, the performance of the Church must be seen to flow from the conduct of Jesus. The New Testament record of Jesus' "way of being in the world" offers elements that disclose what I must call the "trinitarian horizon" of his experience and action. In this context, one very fruitful line of enquiry would lead us to consider the meaning of the prayer of Jesus, — especially as Luke treats of it (e.g. 3,21; 5,16; 6,12; 9,18 . . .). His all but isolated character of communing with God leads to the further questions of Jesus' exclusive experience of the Father, the signature of which is the "Abba" prayer (Cf. Mt 6,9; Lk 11,2; Mt 11,25 . . . Lk 23,34; 23,46). In the light of this, there is some indication of how Jesus experienced himself as Son, enjoying with the Father, an exclusive reciprocity of knowledge, so strikingly and surprisingly expressed in Mt 11,27. In the living sense of this relationship we can locate his sense of ultimate authority, his consciousness of being the representative of the many, and sent as the bringer of salvation, his scandalous solidarity with outcasts, the sense of himself as central to God's plan and as the one desired by the prophets and wise men, his union with the suffering, and his place in the eucharistic gift of the New Covenant.

As a counterpoint to his experience of Sonship is his awareness of himself as possessed and impelled by the Holy Spirit (not that we need to say that he made the Holy Spirit a special object of his teaching). His mission is governed by the impulse of this Spirit, a theme so dear to Luke. He contests the allegation that his actions are motivated by some spirit other than that of the Holy Spirit, and warns about a blasphemy against the spirit of his activity, of forgiving, healing and setting free. J. D. G. Dunn sums up his research into the experience of Jesus: "Jesus thought of himself as God's Son and as anointed by the eschatological Spirit, because in prayer he experienced God as Father, and in ministry he experienced the power to heal which he could only understand as the power of the end-time and as an inspiration to proclaim a message . . . as the gospel of the end-time". (*Jesus and the Spirit,* SCM, 1975, p.67). Whilst I concede the deep hermeneutical problems in Dunn's work, the elements are there to reflect on.

For trinitarian theology the issue turns on the nature of the data on which we reflect: what we have been suggesting in these few sentences is that the "given" in the New Testament is not a doctrine, nor even primarily an understanding. Rather we are challenged by an experience disclosed in a historical way of being and acting in the world, an experience fundamentally, of God: such an experience would always be the despair of reflection, for all available categories are stretched beyond their native scope. The second comment on the scriptural experience of God adds a further refinement to our task of grounding our trinitarian reflection in Scripture.

(b) The line of research that I indicated above (eg. Muhlen, Cooke, Dunn, et al.) is surely promising. But I have one reservation: it can tend to make us forget the *movement* of New Testament experience especially as it is instanced in the action and preaching of Jesus. For he taught no new theology. That God was loving, merciful, faithful and just could scarcely be questioned by a devout Jew. What Jesus did was to involve God, through his action, in a disconcerting subversive way in regard to the theo-political world of his time. He added no new thoughts about God, but by his action raised the question, how was the true God to be practically honoured?

The spirit which possessed him inspired him, for example, to heal on the Sabbath (Mk 3,1-6), and to associate so acceptingly with the "irreligious". The perfection he demanded was not that of a more refined calculation of the law, but that of mercy, that gift of "the impossible new chance" for one's brethren, one's enemies, one's persecutors (Mt 5,48); in this his followers were to imitate the perfection of God. But this impossible new chance was so subversive of the law and the theocratic order of the established religious world: "They immediately held counsel with the Herodians against him, how to destroy him" (Mk 3,6). For he involved God in a liberating action on behalf of the poor and sinners: "The Sabbath was made for man . . .", as a symbol of divine liberation, not as an instrument of oppression forbidding even the healing of a "daughter of Abraham" (Lk 15,16).

Such a contestation on behalf of the truth of God leads to the cross. The "rulers" understood this as the justice of God on the blasphemer. Jesus understood it as the way to honour the Father (Cf Lk 23,36-39).

Jesus' subversion of the closed religious ordering of society on behalf of God came to a uniquely intense kind of expression. For as he involved God in this way, he invoked him, with all the implications of exclusivity, as "my Father". His opponents deemed his action diabolic, whilst Jesus presented his actions as inspired by the Holy Spirit. The cross was the result, — and the resurrection the divine legitimation of his way of acting on behalf of the One True God.

Despite the vulnerability of this approach to a crudely anti-institutional prejudice, it remains basically plausible. The trinitarian symbolism (the action of the prophetic Son, under the inspiration of the Holy Spirit, involving the Father) is a powerful condensed expression of God's liberating activity in the world. To this degree, the scriptural foundation of trinitarian theology demands that it be truly a theology of liberation.[2]

(c)   Our final scriptural point deals with the New Testament's perception of the Trinity as a problem. I am not implying that the Trinity was foremost a problem for the early Christian communities; for rather obviously the dominant theme is the celebration and confession of the grace imparted to mankind through the coming of the Son and the sending of the Spirit. The triadic pattern emerges in an effort to give full expression to the absolute gift of God, and this, apparently, from a very early time. True, there is not much to compare with the single lapidary trinitarian (probably baptismal) formula of Mt 28,19). Yet there is an abundance of triadic and tri-partite expressions (e.g. Gal 3,11f; 4,6; 2 Cor 1,21f; 3,3; Phil 3,3; Col 1,6ff; 1 Pt 1,1ff; Tt 3,4f; Hb 10,29 etc. . . .). These are not formal credal statements, yet they do indicate the early Christian belief in Father, Son and Spirit in a simple and uncomplicated way. These early writers speak of adoring the Father, confessing the Son, acting in the Spirit, without any hesitation or misgiving. They seem to assume that this is the way to speak about the faith they experience and that it will be readily understood in this way by their hearers.

But a more "systematic" consciousness is evident in John. Certainly, there are no technically dogmatic or metaphysical terms, but there does seem to be a co-ordinated doctrine. John seems aware of a special need to correlate the components of Christian faith in reference to the Father, Son and Holy Spirit. I cannot even outline here the general structure of his doctrine about the Word "from the beginning" who is alone the "interpreter of the Father" (Jn 1). However Jn 16,12-16 reveals an all but scholastic sensitivity to the need for a precise way of speaking: "I have yet many things to say to you but you cannot bear them now. When the Spirit of truth comes, he will guide you into all truth, for he will not *speak on his own authority,* but *whatever he hears he will speak,* for he will declare the things that are to come. *He will glorify me,* for *he will take what is mine* and declare it to you. *All that the Father has is mine;* therefore *I said he will take what is mine* and declare it to you".

The least that can be said is that John is aware of a problem in the rhetoric of faith and opens the way to facing that problem and solving it. The dogmatic concentration of the five centuries following John's writings will bring about the concerted effort of Christian realism to define what the real dimensions of faith are. This would be quite anachronistic in the life-world of the New Testament; but the dynamics of a trinitarian theology have begun.

All I have attempted in the desperate brevity of this outline is to indicate some lines of research into the scriptural foundations of trinitarian theology. I would be happy to conclude that the New Testament presents us less with a doctrine about the Trinity, and more with a way of thinking and feeling what God must keep meaning for "us men and our salvation".

---

1. Quoted in J. Moltmann, "The Trinitarian History of God", *Theology* LXXVIII (Jan 1975) 632-646, p. 633, note 2.

2. Cf. Ch. Duquoc, *Dieu Different. Essai sur la symbolique trinitaire* (Cerf: Paris 1977).

6

Trinitarian symbolism and the religious imagination

IT MIGHT appear quaint to intrude the theme of the Trinity into a psycho-therapeutical context. If it does, part of the explanation might be that religious doctrine has become so divorced from affectivity. Trinitarian doctrine is couched in the classical and, today, probably misleading, terms of three divine persons in one divine nature, Father, Son and Holy Spirit. It may well represent a logical coordination of Christian discourse; but unless you are theologically initiated, and therefore alert to the tacit sense of mysteries always exceeding propositional expression, you may not find much in such a doctrine to lift the mind or expand the heart. You may well fear, in the highly complex framework of Christian communication, that doctrine, affect and conduct have been wedged in separate pigeon holes.

The theologically minded will try to assuage your fear. The tradition of faith is a highly complex musical score. There are many rich chords in the basic theme of faith: the harmony of doctrine and experience is there if you listen carefully enough. If you don't then the affective tones of Christian experience might seem like archaic fibrillations of the human spirit in a limitless impersonal universe. If you do listen carefully, the deep notes of doctrine are heard as an affirmation of the ultimate character of the universe with which our experience ultimately harmonises. In other words, the Trinity, for all its seeming abstract complexity, is actually a statement about reality as it grounds and encompasses our existence. The single word "God" is not sufficient by itself to refer to this ultimate reality. For Christian faith takes its rise from the fundamental experiences of Jesus living and dying as Son to bring about the Kingdom of the One he addressed as Father. It lives from the experience of a Holy Spirit which possessed Jesus and is communicated to the community of those who follow him.

The consequence is that it has elaborated its experience of God through a series of relational terms. We cannot affirm the reality of God in simple absolute terms. The mystery of the saving God has to be narrated: the Father utters his Word/Son into the world, and then communicates the Spirit of love that unites them both. Thus God is conceived as Father, Son and Spirit, in a love-life of mutual self-giving. The divine three possess their identity only by being related to the others. In this sense, the ultimate reality of the universe is a communion of ecstatic unlimited love: "God is Love" 1 Jn 4,8). God gives what is most intimate and essential to his own identity (Son and Spirit) into all the risk and vulnerability of the human world (1 Jn 4,7-12). If that is true, it is very true; and if it is held to be very true, then it must resonate very deeply in the psyche of anyone who believes it to be so. It must make a difference, this manner of envisioning the character of the ultimate ground and goal of the universe of our experience.

And yet . . .? At this point the psychologically initiated must suspect a certain naivete in leaving any account of Christian faith as objective and as direct as that. The professional therapists would instinctively feel that any account of faith in God must be far more aware of the intricacies and dynamics of the world of affect. Truth we may well search for, know, believe, delight in and praise. But true cognitive meanings do not directly become constitutive of our inner-most identity and feelings. The greatest comprehensions of life's meaning are wrapped up with a subtle history of feeling, with all the reactions of desire, fear, anger, confidence or diffidence. For these feelings are the momentum of our psychic lives. Truth is of supreme value, certainly; and we must always tend toward it. But to suppose that it occurred in easy untrammelled directness would be very naive.

If truth and especially religious truth were not a concern, then even the most serious discussions are little more than the antics of a public or private imagination whereby we gesticulate, this way or that, in the ebb and flow of stimulus and response. The whole process would in fact be devoid of any honest outreach or real reference. On the other hand, we must be content with the world of affect. Feelings enlarge or stunt our capacities for the real, indeed our capacity for God. Diseased feelings exercise their subtle, violent effect as they feed our private demons and enclose us in an increasingly alienated and isolated world.

The classic figure in unmasking the destructive power of affect was, of course, Freud. He stands with the other great masters of suspicion, those founding fathers of modern culture, who attacked the world of religion as a perversion of reality. Darwin, with his evolutionary theory and, later, his evolutionary myth, challenged religious imagination not to dissociate itself from the biophysical developmental process of the world. Human beings did not drop down from heaven to preside as pure spirits over the material world; they are part of a vast cosmic development and immersed in a history of evolving life. Marx, too, shocked the naive religious imagination: he dramatised the cultural and economic dynamics of how our "gods" were nothing but a mythological manipulation of reality to serve our own self-interests, — to keep our position safe in an unjust society. And Nietzsche, (a powerful influence in early Australian literature) inveighed against Christianity for its hatred of life and beauty. He understood such faith to be born out of resentment and mistrust. For him, it inverted the true human scale of values; it demeaned power, liberty, all vital forces, to glorify dependence, lowliness and a negative attitude to all that was best in us.

But Freud's criticism of the religious imagination was the most subtle of all. The acknowledgement of such a complexity might excuse me from attempting a full account of it — especially when so many good treatments of this question exist.[1] Of course, his criticism was itself criticised, right from the beginning, in the larger "spiritual" proportions of, say, Otto Rank and Carl Jung — as today, in the writings of

Ernest Becker (e.g. *The Denial of Death,* New York, The Free Press, 1975) and Victor Frankl (*Man's Search for Meaning,* New York, Washington Square Press, 1970) etc. as in all the modern psychological theories which allow that a hopeful, courageous search for ultimate meaning is not necessarily a symptom of mental disease.

After all, we can repress our "eternal longings" just as effectively as we might repress our instinctual drives.

Nonetheless, Freud's criticism is there, and it is a classic one. He took over the general "projection theory" of Ludwig Feuerbach. This understood the notion of God as a result, positively or negatively, of wishful thinking: the primitive or diseased imagination objectified itself in religious terms. These gave expression to what was unrealised or unresolved in human freedom. What Freud added to Feuerbach was a psychological reinforcement of the projection theory. He provided clinical terms to explain how God was made in man's image. His main works are: *The Future of an Illusion* (1927); *Civilisation and its Discontents* (1930); *Moses and Monotheism* (1939). For him religious notions were not "precipitates of experience or the end-results of thinking". They are "illusions, fulfilments of the oldest, strongest and most urgent wishes of mankind. The secret of their strength lies in the strength of those wishes". (*The Future of an Illusion,* p. 30).

What are these wishes which give such strength to religious notions? They arise out of the infant-like helplessness of all human beings in their confrontation with a strange and overwhelming universe. Consequently, we human beings long for protection from life's dangers, for justice in an unjust society, for life beyond the extinction of death, for a knowledge of the beginning and end of our history, for the integration of the bodily and psychic in our personal existence. To quote Freud again: "The unclear inner perceptions of our own psychic apparatus stimulate illusions which are naturally projected outward, and, characteristically, into the future, and into a hereafter. Immortality, retribution, the whole hereafter are such representations of our psychological interior . . . a

61

psychomythology". (From a letter quoted in H. Küng, *Does God Exist?*, Vintage Books, New York, 1981, p. 283).

In individual and cultural instances, these wishes are rooted in the conflicts of childhood as they take the form of a "father-complex", that desire for an omnipotent father who might protect the little human being from the threatening powers of nature and fate. The infantile imagination creates a paternal deity which needs both to be feared and placated if the human psyche is to have some protection against the darkness of fate and piercing reality of our limitations and creaturehood. Such a God, as Creator is used to banish the terror of nature; and as Saviour, reconciles us to fate and death; whilst as Judge such a divine figure compensates us for all the separations and privations which life, especially the moral life, demands of us.

Thus, religion is wishful thinking. It is essentially the projection of a terrified infantile psyche. It is illusion. As such, it is a psychomythology of the infantile to be deciphered according to the techniques of therapy.

Though Freud allowed for the unlikely possibility that there might be some reality, some truth beyond these illusions, it remained his working conviction that religion, in the individual and in culture, was an obsessional neurosis. It was all basically a manipulation of reality, a flight from the real. What we most needed was to be educated to reality, and so to be cured of the illusory and freed for the limited but actual freedom we had. A scientifically established perception of reality would "leave heaven to angels and sparrows". It would demand that the psychological infant grow up into a responsible adult. "Experience teaches that the world is no nursery". Freud goes on to say, "Our science is no illusion. But an illusion it would be to suppose that what science cannot give us we can get elsewhere" (Küng, p. 286).

Today, I think it is evident that the mechanistic model of science which Freud inherited is simply not good enough.[2] The modern ideal of a total human science in an imperilled world is rather larger and more inclusive than the narrow mechanistic modelling of the late 19th century mind. An enormous world-process of healing and liberation now demands our attention. Any journey inward must be a release for a journey outward to discover new ways of justice and peace-making, if we are to have a human world to share. Still, no matter what the faith and hope any of us may have maintained or discovered, Freud's critique of religion keeps on having a classic relevance. For there is no one of us who, having embarked on the exploration of faith, has not found in himself/herself the escapist and manipulative tendencies of which the great analyst speaks. We can learn from him to enter more critically into that exploration of the ultimately real, and to undergo what John of the Cross called, centuries ago, the "dark night of the soul". Communally, too, we have had to listen to his criticism. For as churches and religious communities we have had to learn to become less conventicles of dependent children finding our security in submission to "those who know"; to become less sectarian in our tendencies to narrow the universe to the problems of our own group identity — and more, I hope, a Church serving and celebrating the universal mystery of Grace.

So, granting all that, I must now get back to the specific topic: trinitarian symbolism and religious imagination. More precisely, what is the psychological impact of invoking God as Father, Son and Holy Spirit?

Before answering this precise question, let me first introduce a distinction. It was provoked by Freud's critique of religion, and is currently used especially by those French authors who have sought to profit from it. Here I have in mind especially Christian Duquoc in his book, *Dieu Différent,* Paris: Cerf 1977. In what follows I am especially reliant on this book, especially pages 83-117. The distinction is made between *l'imaginaire* and *la symbolique.* First, let me stress that, as I implied before, there has been a strange rupture between doctrine and affectivity. Here I am trying to bring the two more realistically together. To this end, it is worth nothing that we cannot express ourselves without images. Even the most refined seemingly abstract doctrines rely on images as the affective underpinning of the more intellectual acts of thinking, reflecting, affirming. Take the case in question: the Trinity, the One God, is affirmed to be Father, Son and Holy Spirit. Such terms are primarily images. Just because they have become ossified or congealed in the religious imagination, it does not mean that they are not somehow in play. The point is, how are they in play? How do they affect the *central* doctrine of Christian faith?

It is at this point that the distinction between *l'imaginaire* and *la symbolique* provides a useful clarification. The first term is used to refer to a religious fantasy world, pretty much as Freud described it — a private psychomythology: it is an ensemble of affects divorced from social communication and interpersonal responsibility. This has been referred to as the realm of the *diabolic*. The original Greek implication of this word is "rending apart", in contrast to *symbolein,* "bringing together": the images, with their affective freight, are kept apart from the responsible critical world of social responsibilities and interpersonal relationships.

In contrast to this, we have *la symbolique,* with its root implications of "bringing together". Symbols are publicly lived images, certainly carrying an appropriate affect, but subject to the critical reality of one's public existence, and inserted into the world of social responsibilities. If you like, the symbolic is an image of self-transcendence, of going beyond oneself to the other, in contrast to the private fantasy world of self-preoccupation and narcissism. The symbolic lives in the social world of speech, with all its critical, clarifying power. It is beholden to the reality of law, too, as the structure of social exchange. There is, in a sense, a critical distance between what is signified and the images that signify. (Duquoc p. 102f).

How is this distinction applied to the trinitarian images of Father, Son and Spirit? Obviously, the most critical, most vulnerable image is that of "Father". A "father-image" floating free in the isolated world of fantasy (*l'imaginaire*) easily ends in fixating the human psyche in an archaic stage of development. Experiencing the limits intrinsic to human existence, that psyche projects on its own inner screen a father-image. This is an instinctive compensation against the pain and separation involved in being human. Psychic development is thus stunted at the expense of the realistic limited freedoms possible to the human condition. Now the image of the "divine father"

64

is the most exquisite product of the immature. In the inevitable process of discovering the obvious limitations of human fathers, neurotics can still find a device for protecting themselves against the demands of reality. For all limitation and weakness is excluded from a paternal divinity. Thus the "religious" can rest secure in their infantilism.

Is the Christian notion of God the Father necessarily such an example of infantile projection? It could be; and for fear of this some might be inclined to try to purge it from the religious psyche. It would be very ingenuous to think that this could take place and have the desired effect. Silence solves nothing. The father-projection would continue to exercise its pathological influence with all the devious creativity of infantile desire, but now aided by silence. And it is interesting to speculate how it attracts into its orbit those other two trinitarian images, Son and Spirit.

For correlated to such a father-image, Jesus as Son is reduced progressively to Jesus the child. Indeed, what is the significance of the image of the divine child in Christian imagination? It is true that, in a few passages in the Gospel, e.g. Mt. 18, 3f, the simplicity and dependence of the child are praised, in contrast to a self-serving, self-enclosed, calculating adulthood. Such instances have been endlessly employed to justify a certain kind of infantilism in Christian spirituality. The place of the Divine Infant in the Christian imagination would certainly have elicited a self-congratulatory chuckle from Dr. Freud who certainly knew "that the world was no nursery".

With God made in the fantasy dimensions of the father-image, the obedience of Jesus, the Son, was portrayed in strangely passive forms. This was a long way from the startling freedom of the Jesus of the Gospels. This odd infantile passivity fed back as a psychic affect into some of the noblest lives of faith. It produced pathologies which produced deep suffering. These occasioned terrible struggles to find wholeness and hope. I have in mind here especially Thérèse of Lisieux, whose religious name was Thérèse of the Infant Jesus. Her life is a wonderful document of this struggle to be truly adult in faith (Cf. Ida F. Görres, *The Hidden Face,* Burns & Oates: London, 1959). The path of this bourgeois French girl to an adult and magnificent faith, living and dying as she did, in the lifetime of Freud, is still too little studied by the disciplines we discuss here. She broke out of the pattern of what was expected: indeed, those closest to her, her sisters in family and in religious life, so intent were they on keeping intact her bland childlike image, that they touched up her photo, and edited out of the records the more dramatic expressions of her spiritual struggle. But that is another, longer and very interesting story. Suffice it for our purposes to say that, in Christian affectivity, the dynamics of the "father-projection" can be so strong that the basic trinitarian symbolism of Father and Son are drawn into such a manipulation of reality as supporting it rather than purifying it in any way.

Along similar lines, the Christian symbol of the Holy Spirit can be drawn into the primitive fantasy world of *l'imaginaire.* It too can be pressed into service to justify a range of pathologies masquerading as religious faith. The classic reference here is Ronald Knox's *Enthusiasm,* (Oxford Clarendon Press, 1950). In the biblical context, Paul's letter to the "spirit-filled" Corinthians is the essential reference: apparently these colourful cosmopolitan early Christian converts were inclined to justify an almost orgiastic self-indulgence by appealing to the influence of the Spirit. Probably, some of us have been forced to express some reservations about Pentecostal and Charismatic groups in recent years. At their best, they witnessed to an ecstatic and liberating dimension of religious experience — something we all need. At their worst, there was evidence of a sort of irrepressible irresponsibility, along with strong indications of emotional manipulation, sectarian eccentricity and doctrinaire anti-intellectualism.

Such negative aspects of the "Spirit-experience" are demonstrably a flight from reality. They result from the symbol of the Spirit being detached from a social and interpersonal context; and this left an isolated affectivity to "blow where it willed".

We have to concede, then, that these central Christian symbols of the divine can be drawn into the manipulating dynamics of fantasy, *l'imaginaire.* As a corrective to this, I will now sketch, very briefly, how these symbols are meant to function in a Christian faith critically concerned with the real. This is the realm of *la symbolique*: the responsible, liberating, affective setting of the theological images, Father, Son and Holy Spirit. I know that theology is never psychotherapy in the professional clinical sense. Still, a critical theology is therapeutic. It can assist the religious psyche to purify itself of the more obvious neurotic propensities which tend to bedevil all those who dare to enter into the adventure of faith.

In the first place, recall that the basic way of naming and invoking God occurs in a social context. The leading reality is not some generalised "father-image" of the divine — as though God were somehow already known, and was sending some further private communication to believers in the words of his unique Son, and warming the believing heart with the consolations of his Holy Spirit. The scriptural reality is quite different. No one doubts that Jesus did invoke God in an unconventional familiar way, as *Abba*. But the setting of such an invocation is important. Jesus is not teaching theology. No devout Jew doubted that God was living and merciful. The whole force and energy of Jesus' life was to show what this meant in practice. The Gospels reveal him as the living parable of the divine mystery. He is depicted as a man of action and startling freedom. He works for and proclaims a new order of reality, which is somehow mysteriously present already in him and what he says and does. This new order of reality he named *the Kingdom of God*. It was a reality far more universal and inclusive, far more gracious and inviting, far more world-shattering, too, than anything even the most devout of his own people were expecting. It was this reality that he embodied and enacted. He was scandalously involved with the excommunicates and "no hopers" of his day. His conviviality as both guest and host with the disreputable was proverbial: "Why does your master eat with publicans and sinners?" (Mk 1, 21—3, 6.) How does he dare to perform works of healing on the sacred day of the Sabbath? Why does he criticise the administration of the temple? Such questions were asked about him; and there were those who considered that he was possessed by the devil, so radically

67

new was the sense of reality that emanated from him (Mk 3, 20-30).

His defence was always reduced to this: he was acting in the name of limitless mystery and mercy and grace, the God who really is involved with a broken and lost humanity. Jesus is not so much speaking about God. He rather involved God in the way he healed, drove out demons, celebrated with sinners, offered forgiveness, called his followers and told his parables. It is not an exaggerated expression to say that he "freed God to be God", enabled God to break out of the constrictions of the religious system that had in a sense captured him. That is where the freedom and the fascination of this Jesus was most remarkable: "Amen, I say to you . . ." The way of the living God was revealed in him to be a path of freedom and new hope for those who were most oppressed and hopeless.

Implicitly, Jesus contested all the inhuman accretions attached to our notions of God. In our terms, he opposed a new and gracious reality to a neurotic self-absorbed world of religious fantasy. In the thrust of his action on behalf of real human beings, especially those who were most broken and lost, he involved God as "Father". The implication was that the One so invoked was a universal life-giving mystery which was the foundation of Jesus' relationship to the hopeless, just as it was meant to be the foundation of our relationships to one another: "Be merciful as your heavenly Father is merciful". Such a God was the God of true freedom and human belonging. Such a God was not to be invoked as a religious force somehow sparing those who invoked him the painful reality of freedom. There would be no legions of angels to protect Jesus from the consequences of his dedication to such a Father. If the world was to change, if God was to reign, it would not be through a miraculous manipulation of reality. It would have to come about through the energies and mysteries of a self-giving love. The result was the Cross. The love of God had to be vulnerable if it was ever to be real.

So we conclude: the images of Father and Son in the Gospels are symbols of the God of social responsibilities and interpersonal love. The Son embodies, for Christians, the form of a non-calculating compassionate involvement with and for the other. The Father is the symbol of the universal mystery: the space, as it were, in which believers can live and move and find themselves bound in a common destiny and a common hope for everyone and everything.

Now we must make reference to the third symbol of the Holy Spirit. Any easy symmetry of a God enclosed in his own being, of the Father fulfilled in the Son, or the Son totally fulfilled in the Father, is challenged by this third symbol. The Spirit, as it were, occurs between the Father and the Son, the Spirit of the both. In a sense, this Spirit stands for deep realities of the divine freedom, of the divine capacity to draw all creation into the fundamental relationship of Father and Son. The Spirit is divine excess and ecstasy, God as an inclusive outgoing reality.

In the Gospels, the Spirit is presented as the Holy Breath, the one in whose power Jesus acts to drive out evil spirits as they oppress and possess the afflicted. It was this Spirit of liberated and liberating life which Jesus promised to those who believed in him. As early Christians reflected on this Spirit of new life, as they experienced its energies, they came to express it in four main ways, each of which is relevant to the understanding of Christian therapy and pathology (Duquoc, 106-111).

First of all, the Spirit is a divine energy. "You shall receive power when the Spirit comes to you" (Ac 1,8). In the gift of the Spirit, the inertia of the past is overcome. Reality is now a new creation. Enslavement and fear yields to freedom. The Spirit is the living principle of hope (Gal 5,5). This Spirit, with all the allied symbolisms of wind, fire, fountain of living water, is conceived of as breaking the binding power of the past to open believers to the reality of the new. Psychologically speaking, such a Spirit symbolises a break in the logic of infantile desire. For this would seek its satisfaction in the secure repetition of the round of untroubled familiar existence. Against this, the Holy Spirit is "the breath of fresh air", of the radically new and unpredictable. It is the Spirit of exodus, of what is not yet, of openness to the promise of existence. There is no going back to an untroubled paradise. A new heaven and a new earth are in the making.

Secondly, the Spirit symbolises freedom. "Where the Spirit of the Lord is, there is freedom" (2 Cor 3,17). This certainly does not mean a facile negation of all law, even if the Spirit is the new interior law of love. An abolition of all law is symptomatic of the unreality of infantile desire; an archaic emotional pattern. The Spirit-symbol in the logic of Christian realism makes us think of freedom in a way that negates both legalism and libertinism. It allows both law and liberty to play their part in reality of social exchange. The fruits of this Spirit, in the words of Paul, are "love . . . and self-control" (Gal 5,23). If the Sabbath is made for man and not man for the Sabbath, it does not mean that the Sabbath is abrogated. It is relocated as a positive human and religious value. The Spirit of Christian realism de-absolutises the law, but does not destroy it as a necessary social structure. With such limits placed on infantile desire, human co-existence is rendered possible. If such a Spirit-inspired freedom leads the believer to be free with God as "Father" (Rom 8,15), as participating in the character of the Son, it is always in the context of living in a genuinely fraternal world.

Thirdly, the Spirit inspires communion and the unity of love (Gal 15,22; 1 Cor 12). But such unity in the Spirit is not conceived of in terms of a repressive uniformity of undifferentiated symbiosis — as the world of infantile desire might envisage. When the Spirit comes at Pentecost, each nation still speaks its own language. Though Paul sees us all possessing the same Spirit, individuals have different gifts in the one Body of Christ (1 Cor 12, 4ff). And even if, in Christ, there is no Jew or Greek, slave or free, male or female, this is not the result of a monomanic desire to reduce everything to a primitive uniformity. Differences in fact remain, but not as destructive conflicts and alienated powerblocks. They are polarities, but now in a newer, richer context. Similarly, in the name of the Spirit, Paul imposes silence on those inclined to glossallic excesses (1 Cor 14,1-20). Such inspired languages must lead to positive communication, not private indulgence. It would seem in all this that the unity of the

Spirit subverts the infantile self-project by leading the believer to accept the reality of the other as a grace not as a threat.

Fourthly, the Spirit leads to recall or inspired memory: "The Spirit will teach you all things and bring to mind all that I have said to you" (Jn 14,26). The Spirit acts by conforming the faithful to the objective reality of the Son, to cause them to follow the way of Jesus in service and self-sacrifice for the other (Gal 5, 22ff). It counteracts the desire to escape into some spiritual realm out of the exigencies of an interpersonal world. It offers no cheap grace. It moves us to follow the way of the crucified, with all the reality of the many dyings implied in that. In short, the Holy Spirit of the new creation, of unity and freedom continually recalls the believer to the reality of the real world in which the Son was crucified and the Father refuses to exercise any other power than that of self-surrendering love.

Such then is a brief outline of a theological approach to trinitarian symbolism. It criticises the manipulating dynamics of infantile fantasy which, of course, remains present in all of us. It is not psychotherapy; but, I hope, reflections such as this might suggest ways in which different disciplines might reflect together for the promotion of human integrity, human worth, and the freedoms which we desire but find so imperilled from within and without.

---

1. For the documentation of this section, I am indebted to H. Küng, *Does God Exist?*, Vintage Books: New York, 1981, pp. 262-304.

2. See, for example, Fritjof Capra, *The Turning Point* (London: Flamingo, 1982) espec. 182-193.

7

Approaches to a theology of the Holy Spirit

THERE are three good reasons to opt for the way of "approaching" in this context:

First, the Mystery of the Spirit. The "Holy Breath" precedes and goes beyond the Word, to blow where it will. It is a gift originating in the divine freedom. It is a divine surprise often catching believers unawares, a universal presence not constrained by any of our particularities; and an eschatological energy never contained by the norms and systems of this present age. So, to "approach" implies both a kind of adoration and a respect for the subject matter.

Secondly, the proliferation of theologies. I cannot pretend to master the now immense literature on the Spirit, e.g., the writings of Congar, Muhlen, Coffey, Durrwell, Bouyer, Dunn, Brown, Taylor, Jüngel, Hill. To "approach" implies a readiness to take part in a conversation rather than a desire to stop this very complex and rich exchange with some pretence of a fixed and finished theology.

Thirdly, I believe that here, above all, one's approach determines the vitality and the breadth of one's theology. By pointing to the following avenues of "approach", I hope to liberate a theology of the Spirit to a larger breadth and a more obvious creativity. The context is as important as the content which, in this case, might be inherently quite slender: for what can you say about the Holy Spirit directly? How much can you expect to express the divine Surprise and the divine Gift? Admittedly, we can say quite a lot about our complex human consciousness of the Spirit, as it strives to elaborate what it experiences, and to serve the Mystery which both penetrates and escapes its horizon.

The present Situation of Theology of the Spirit

It is commonly admitted that we of the Latin West have not had a particularly rich or profound theology of the Spirit. The Spirit is very much "The Third Divine Person" — a kind of afterglow once the important things have been said on the Father and the Son. Systematic theology tended to make use of a fairly impoverished version of the psychological image. In this, the Son is related to the divine Word of God's understanding of Himself and all creation, and the Spirit is related to God's loving of himself and all things thus understood. To many, even those well versed in Scholastic theology, this seemed very abstract and even arbitrary, not really capable of illuminating the variety of the biblical data or the dimensions of human experience. Theology appeared to be locked in one model. This is a good model, I shall contend, but no more expressing the whole reality than a nautical chart expresses the reality of the Barrier Reef.

Further, against this rigid and impoverished theology, there arose three notable objections. One from the Eastern Orthodox tradition which, even during Vatican II, reproached the Latin West with Christomonism and with that subordination of the Spirit of which the *Filioque* is still the emblem. Another objection arose from the charismatic experience. This released, ambiguously at times, a consciousness of the vitality of the Spirit's presence in the Christian community. And the third objection came from a new ecclesial awareness of the "Cornelius conundrum" (Ac 10), the experience of the Spirit's insistence on administering the Church by prompting it to discern the unsettling indications of the "Signs of the Times" at the expense of "ecclesiastical business as usual" administering the Spirit to oil the machinery of routine Church life.

These challenges provoked a more epicletic theology which presents the life of the Church in terms of adoring and invoking the Spirit as the fundamental condition for its action.

In this sense, the Spirit is the first divine person in the experience of the Church rather than the third divine person of our dogmatic systems.

This new sense of the Spirit necessarily provoked a new theology affecting the understanding of the Church as a communion and a mission. It is having influence in the formulation of Christology in which Christ is more clearly presented as the one uniquely anointed by the Spirit.

Though the present situation called forth a new appreciation of the Spirit, it was not without resources. The most obvious resource is the flowering of Scriptural studies over the past decades. But there are two other resources which may strike the reader as surprising. First, traditional trinitarian theology, especially in its modern adaptations, say, in Rahner and Lonergan. We had here, at least in schematic fashion, a profound theology of God as *Agape*. The divine persons were conceived of as "subsisting relationships", so that the divine mystery was presented as a communion of ecstatic, self-giving, relational persons. To be the Father meant to be totally "Sonward", in the Spirit. To be Son meant to be totally "Fatherward" in the same Spirit. To be Spirit meant to be totally from and for the Father and the Son. Divine personal life was essentially relational. It consisted in mutual self-giving. Its unity was a differentiated communion. True, it was not the "Process Theology" that would appear this century, but a "Procession Theology", with the divine processions the origin, form and goal of the whole created process. This quite traditional scheme is a powerful corrective to the notion of the "self-sufficient Absolute" of Greek philosophical tradition. Further, it subverts the notion of any absolute monism which might be invoked for a political or ecclesiastical ideology. It continues to challenge the abstract benevolence of the Deity of the Enlightenment. For our purposes, it opens the way for an appreciation of the Spirit as a personal mode of divine relationality drawing the whole of creation and history into the intercommunication of Father and Son.

Following the more modern biblical stress on the *economia,* this relational character of the divine Mystery began to be expressed in historical terms (e.g. Von Balthasar, Rahner).

74

The relational character of the divine persons is found in the intent of each to glorify the other: the Father refuses any identity in the world save that expressed in the Son: "This is my beloved Son. Hear him" (Mk 9,7). The Son rejects any worldly identity save that of being totally for the Father (e.g. Mt 4,1-12). And both Father and Son, in their openness to the freedom of human history, refuse any presence in the world, after the resurrection, save that of their common Spirit (Jn 16, 13ff). The Spirit, in turn, acts in the full force of his being to lead all to the Father through the Son (Jn 14,26; 16,13ff). Thus the traditional scheme was opened to include history in a more explicit manner. The immanent and the economic Trinity interpenetrate.

A second surprising source is the traditional Marian devotion amongst Catholics and Orthodox (e.g. Ss. Grignon de Montfort, Maximilian Kolbe, Alphonsus di Liguori.) In the milieu of the Catholic tradition, it has been the role of Mary, in some sense, to carry a deep theology of the Spirit. She was understood to be pre-eminently the temple of the Spirit, uniquely gifted by the Spirit, almost an "incarnation of the Spirit" (Maximilian Kolbe). It is she who brings forth Christ. She is the foremost witness to him. She finds all her meaning in him. She prays with all believers. She leads them to Christ. She forms them in her extended motherhood. She lives at the heart of the Church. She is the "mediatrix of all graces". And for millions of believers, she causes the mystery of God to be experienced in a special tenderness and intimacy. In bringing God near as Love, she subverts any exclusively masculine designation of the Divine.

Admittedly, such a series of statements brims with confusion. But not all confusions are superficial or unhealthy. The whole extraordinary, perhaps extravagant and overloaded, Catholic experience of Mary remains as an invitation to a more differentiated Catholic theology, in the direction of a deeper grasp of the Spirit manifest in Mary and indeed in all the saints. Now Mary as the Mother of Jesus, the Mother of Christ, the first of the redeemed, will, I must presume, always keep her place in the heart of faith. Nonetheless, the Marian phenomenon in Catholic piety is an invitation to, and occasion for Catholic theology to create a richer theology of the Spirit. For the Marian mystery has, for long centuries, been implicitly carrying such a theology, on the level of piety, devotion, popular experience.

So I make mention of these two resources which could be overlooked. The "inter-connection of mysteries" leads to a deeper theological exploration of each aspect of faith. I hope, in this instance, it will lead to richer theology of the Spirit.

I will now, very briefly, make seven points, each of which provokes its own type of question.

1. A More Spiritual Theology: Is the Spirit "at the Foundations?"

I am asking here whether or not it is simply a matter of coming up with a new theological tract (e.g. Pneumatology) to replace, say, the traditional treatise on Grace: as though what was previously left out, can now be put in; as though all you would need to do with Hans Küng's *On Being a Christian* would be to add a chapter on the Spirit, and that would be that — (despite his disclaimer in note 80, pg. 686). All theological themes interconnect and condition one another. Still, I am looking for something deeper than the mere addition of the fresh theme of the Spirit to the theological system.

To speak more technically, the mystery of the Spirit would seem to belong to the very foundation of any theology. There is no contact with the reality of Christ save in the Spirit. There is no knowledge of God as "Abba", save in the Spirit. There is no specifically Christian level of morality save in the power of the Spirit's love. There is no genuine Christian dialogue or ecclesial relationship except in the vital field of the Spirit 1 Cor 2,10-16; Gal 5,16-26; Rom 5,5 . . .).

Now if such assertions have any biblical or theological warrant, then they are very true. If they are very true, then theological method, theological style, theological art, expression and praxis must somehow evince the presence of the Spirit. For theology, in a critical manner, must appropriate its procedures as an exploration not only *of* the Spirit, but *in* the Spirit. It must be a pedagogy serving the pedagogy of the Spirit. It may begin to conceive of itself as a consciousness-raising entry into the milieu of the Spirit. As such it would be an activity of the "spiritual man" who, in a conscious yielding to the Spirit, seeks to penetrate the "gifts bestowed on us by God" (1 Cor 2,12).

No doubt many readers would be already shuddering at the prospect of a cloyingly pietistic theology — as I would. I do not think the mystery of the Spirit is well served by an uncritical piety or a pseudo-mystical silliness which refuses to think. Still, the challenge does not go away. Of course, the proliferation of courses in "spiritual theology" is partially meeting this challenge, e.g. theologies of prayer, mysticism, discernment, religious experience. But these seem often to operate with a presumed permission to not push things too far intellectually; and they are very wary of secular academic criteria. The deeper challenge is not only to be intelligent in this area, but as T. S. Eliot would say, to be very intelligent: to respect, critically, sensitively, the affective, the moral, the religious exigencies of our consciousness along with the intellectual demands. Each level reveals the presence of the Spirit: as a gift of a new energy of loving; a new range of values; a new sense of God; a new horizon of understanding. If Luther said, "Experientia facit theologum" (experience makes the theologian), we might extend that formula to mean "Spiritus facit theologum" (The Spirit makes the theologian).

Could it be that we have all practised theology more as a discipline than as a charism? Could it be that we have pursued an incarnational model of theology at the expense of the Pneumatic? By offering words to the Word that he be incarnate in the structures of intelligence as it functions in acceptable and even controllable cultural systems, have we failed to offer our creative spirits to the Spirit in order to become artists and poets of new ranges of meaning? A question of emphasis, surely; but still a question. How, then, can our theology be a Spiritual praxis intent not only on the understanding of the role of the Spirit but of operating within his all-pervasive presence? In what sense is the Spirit, the "first divine person" in our theological method?

2. Experiencing the Real: Is There Room for the Spirit?

How does our fundamental experience and understanding of the *real* influence a theology of the Spirit? It would seem that any understanding of Being as statically achieved perfection, as essential form, as hierarchically ordered and articulated grades of perfection seems from the beginning to counter a very vital sense of the Spirit as a pervasive, all-inspiring relational presence. Whereas a philosophy that would privilege the dynamic, the relational, the emergent, the becoming, the maternal, as fundamental categories strikes me as offering more promising terms for a more inspiring theology of the Holy Breath. In this context, let me make three points:

a) *A more evolutionary understanding*: I want to avoid un-necessary complexities here, so I will state the matter as simply as possible. Take, for example, one's conception of human being in the cosmos. If, say, we think of human existence as a half-way point up the ladder of an ascending scale of per-fection, with God at the top and prime matter on the bottom, that will structure theology in a certain way when you deal with Christ and the Spirit. This "ladder model" of the cosmos, with its capacity to be elaborated in terms of a classical philo-sophy of form, essence, nature and act, will allow for a strong theology of the incarnation in a certain context, e.g. Chalcedon. God, at the top of the ladder, comes down as it were to make our ascent possible. But the role of the Spirit in this descent-ascent movement is not easily grasped; nor are realities of history and cosmogenesis easy to express.

On the other hand, if I conceive of human existence in more evolutionary and historical terms, say as an arrowhead of consciousness emerging out of the undifferentiated becoming of the cosmos, to direct it, in intelligence and freedom, to further goals, then a different theology of Christ and his Spirit results. God, the all-actuating reality is not so much on the top of the ladder, but is the *Dynamics* hidden in all the becom-ing; the creative force enabling all being to transcend itself into a greater becoming; a greater unity, consciousness and freedom. Now such an evolutionary model is more hospitable to the biblical suggestion of the Spirit working in all creation (Gn 1; Rom 8). It suggests the presence of the Spirit as the first in our experience, the Holy Breath inspiring a dynamic order, provoking the human spirit into consciousness and freedom; transforming such consciousness into faith and hope; bringing forth, finally, the Christ as the focus for a final kind of human development; diffusing such a development by uniting all to the crucified and risen One in one body. In this way the Spirit brings about a final mutation, intimating the form of the future by even now enabling us to cry "Abba, Father" in the hope that God will be everything to everyone.

In short, the Spirit is the force and breath of cosmogenesis, anthropogenesis, Christogenesis, even theogenesis (in our world). Such a sense of reality opens the way to locate the Spirit more obviously in the realm of the real.

b) *The maternal experience of being*: This point extends the above into another dimension: given that Greek philosophy was a fundamental and indeed classic effort of human intelligence to bring order out of chaos, it developed along certain lines: it tended to privilege the masculine over the feminine by stressing act in regard to potency, form in regard to matter, Logos in regard to mythos, the paternal creative initiative in contrast to the maternal undifferentiated receptivity. In trinitarian theology, it certainly provided categories to explore the Father and the Son, only to remain strangely hesitant and vague regarding the meaning of the Spirit. If we go back before Socrates in this tradition of thought, nature was regarded as the Great Mother. Everything is contained in the womb of becoming. It is in a state of being born within the undifferentiated creativity of a *Natura naturans*. This formless indeterminate all-comprehending "Mother-Nature" held everything within it, all time, all fate. The philosophic break away from undifferentiated wholeness into an articulated critical world-view occurred in the classical period. It strove to conquer time and fate, to establish clear form and logical precision, to promote intellectual and even political independence. The result was that the all-encompassing sense of nature was restricted, to be gradually identified with pure potentiality and prime matter. It was not where God could be found, for nature was identified with potentiality, receptivity, relationality, dependence — with the feminine principle in contrast to the paternal and masculine principle which stood for order, form, act, independence.

This tradition was carried through to theology as we have said. You will find St. Thomas Aquinas, combining so many traditions in his great work, speaking of the defectiveness of the feminine. Though he acknowledged, with all theological thinkers, that God was beyond sexual differentiation, it was most fitting that masculine symbolism be applied to God, e.g. in the generation of the Word, since the feminine implied potentiality and receptivity.

We are now witnessing the breakdown of this patriarchal, paternal, androcentric understanding of reality. As the feminine emerges in its own right, fresh opportunities arise for a theology of the Holy Spirit. Is the Spirit necessarily to be left for consideration only until the male relationships of Father and Son have been explored? Is receptivity, relationality, all-encompassing becoming as anti-divine as we had thought? Is there room for thinking of the Spirit as the divine ground for all unity and distinction, even as the principle of the precise generativity of the Father in regard to the Son, just as Jesus is conceived as Son in the world through the power of the Spirit? Is not the Spirit the deep principle of relational becoming in which we are conceived in Christ to be sons and daughters of the Father?[1]

Again, we are at the point of saying that the Holy Spirit is the first in our experience of the Trinity, the most obvious and all-encompassing, fittingly expressed in a more comprehensive feminine imagery.

c) *A Panentheistic Notion of the Spirit*: (See J. Donceel, "Second Thoughts on the Nature of God", *Thought* (182) Autumn 1971). This point further extends the present line of thought. To put the matter simply, let us start with a simple question: which is the truer statement, given these two positions: i) God is coming to be in the world through the missions of the Son and the Spirit, in a personal and cosmic indwelling; or ii) The world is coming to be in the trinitarian God? I think the latter. Admittedly, we need both types of expression. Yet God is the always greater reality. What is taking place is the "Trinification of the World" (cf. Fred Crowe). As the Father enfolds all in the universal meaning of the Word, and breathes into all creation the universal love of the Spirit, the world is opened to the vision and fulfilment of union with the ultimate Mystery, God, communicated "face to face". God is not contained in the worldly process. He is the ground and goal of the process of that process. All of creation is coming to be in the milieu of trinitarian life. This goes deeper than any affirmation of the identity of the immanent and economic Trinity (cf. Karl Rahner). If one goes along with this way of thinking, the problem is less how the Spirit is in the world but more, how the world is in the Spirit. It suggests that our world is being enfolded into the life-force, the vital field of relationship which the Spirit is. Dare we conceive of the Mystery of the Spirit as the divine Being-in-Love drawing all our freedom, all our loves into itself to make our loving participate in the Love-Life of Father and Son? The world in the Spirit is the eschatological reality; not the Spirit in the world.

I suspect our theology has neglected this eschatological dimension; and with unimaginative timidity tended to imply that the Trinity (containing the strange *tertium quid* of the Spirit) is a theological construction put arbitrarily on our present life — rather than exploring how this present life is a progressive entry into the definite life, that of the Trinity itself: an inhaling of the Holy Breath enabling us slowly to awaken to a new world of relationships, at the centre of which is the Son (and we in him) turned to the Father, and the Father unreservedly turned to the Son.

Of course, these are just three daubs on a large canvas. But, remember, I am asking about our fundamental conception of reality. And I have asked it in three ways: is it dynamic enough? Is it feminine enough? Is it sufficiently eschatological?

3. The Rhetoric of the Spirit: What is the Wording of the Spirit-Experience?

Here I am not concerned immediately with how the Spirit speaks, e.g. as the Spirit witnesses to God as Abba, to Jesus as Lord, in the unutterable groanings of prayer, or in the rather precise directives he gave the early Church. I am directly concerned with the Church's rhetoric about the Spirit in the New Testament. There is the Holy Breath by which the Word is spoken, and there are words about the Holy Breath. I am concentrating on the latter — though, if we have any theological position on the inspiration of the Scriptures, we will hardly forget the former.

Certainly, "rhetoric" is a tricky word; for example, "mere rhetoric" in contrast to a more informed or committed way of speaking. But here I am working with a stronger meaning of rhetoric: certainly the verbal, but that complex creativity which enables us to handle reality, and to celebrate it in all its richness. It is the wording of the real; our speaking of the real into meaning.

Now, our words are meaningful in many ways. Reality is named, invoked, defined, communicated and even formed through our wording. When we read the New Testament, we certainly have a teaching about the Holy Spirit. This is what the disciples in Ephesus lacked (Ac 19,1-3). However, what is far more obvious is that we have in the Scriptures a far more complex rhetoric of meaning, a far more vital celebratory wording than doctrine alone. There is certainly a cognitive content: the Spirit is God's gift, the one who comes to witness to the reality of Christ and so forth. It is more apparent, however, that the biblical rhetoric of the Spirit is constitutive, which is to say it appeals to the minds and hearts of believers to form their consciousness in a certain way: it "constitutes" a new awareness. The Spirit floods the heart with love (Rom 5,5). The Spirit enables the believer to confess Jesus as Lord. The Spirit guides into a deeper knowledge of the mysteries of God. The Spirit is a new principle of interior freedom. As an aspect of Christian identity, as a principle of knowledge and freedom, such a rhetoric is a constitutive meaning.

Then, this complex rhetoric moves into another arc of meaning to be communicative, by forming the community in a certain way. It does this by appealing to a shared experience of the one Spirit; to the diversity of spiritual gifts for the common good; to the one Christ who is the focus of the Spirit's activity. Such a rhetoric aims to build up the community through a communication of what it knows cognitively (i.e. that the Spirit has been given) and by appealing to what it has experienced constitutively (i.e. the indwelling Spirit of the Father and the Son); and by inculcating a shared way of life as "walking in the Spirit" in the freedom of other-regarding love (Ga 5,5).

Finally, the rhetoric of the Spirit turns to effective meaning. The New Testament is not concerned to teach theology, even pastoral theology or spiritual theology; not even exegesis. Its aim is to promote conversion and the work of redemption. In modern terms, it is the language of *praxis* — intent to bring about a faithful Spirit-filled conduct of life, rather than to elaborate a theological product, as it were. And so we are exhorted to live and walk in the Spirit, to receive the fruits of the Spirit, to discern his promptings and obey his direction.

So a complex rhetoric. It does contain cognitive elements; for the Spirit is discerned, named, invoked, received; and a certain clarification of who and what he is, is present, e.g. Jn 16,12-15. But this cognitive element is embedded in a deeper, wider, more practical web of meanings. These deal with what the believer is called to be; what we are together; how we are to nurture community and enter into Christ's mission to the wider world.

A narrowly cognitive approach to the New Testament rhetoric of creative wording can overlook how early this rhetoric took on trinitarian form as it talked of Christian identity, community and action, e.g. 1 Thes 1,1-5. The cognitive did emerge for special consideration, in Jn. 16 as I have just mentioned. Yet it was hundreds of years before the cognitive meaning was clarified and defined, even if, from very early times, Christians were baptised in the trinitarian name (Mt 28,19).

A narrowly cognitive approach, intent on finding an anticipation of Chalcedon and Constantinople, can overlook the plurality of ways of speaking about the whole meaning of the Mystery of Christ. These we could indicate as the rhetoric of fulfilment (he is the "yes" to all God's promises); the rhetoric of participation: he is the vine, we the branches; and the rhetoric of cosmic extension: all things were made in him, through him, for him. So, the point to stress here is this: before we have a precise doctrine of the Spirit we have a New Testament rhetoric, a process of creative wording provoked by experience. This is a way of speaking about the Spirit which any Christian theology must continue. This is above all the expression of a new consciousness "in the Spirit", an experience of intimacy with God as "Abba", that of a fundamental evidence or anointing with the saving truth of Christ; that of being taken into a new field of relationships in the koinonia of the Church. This brings with it an impulse to go where we would resist going, in the courage of mission. The all-transforming gift is worded in many and complex ways, including a sense of the Spirit as the energy of new life and as a new field of relationships, to Christ, to all believers, and even to the whole of creation as it groans in travail.

By hurrying or worrying the cognitive aspect, it is possible to end with a very narrow theology, no longer aware of the original richness of the ways the Spirit was worded.

4. The Narrative of the Spirit: Has Doctrine Stopped the Story?

This point is closely related to the above. For the primary mode in which all this rhetoric operates is narrative. The Gospel is the culmination of the story of God's dealings with creation. It offers us the terms to find the meaning of our own life-stories in the story it tells. The Holy Spirit is the Right Spirit in which such a story is told and heard. And Faith is simply being caught up in the Spirit of the Story.

Apart from being the right atmosphere in which the story of Christ is found to be truly telling, the Spirit is an actor within that story. It is important to recapture a sense of how the mystery of the Spirit is narrated, in its fullness. Otherwise, the danger is to be locked up in one version of the story or restricted to a few dogmatic definitions divorced from the story they were originally intended to serve.

The Gospel story comes within range in different ways, depending on whether we merely overhear it, study it or become part of it. As a story overheard, it is "their story": the story of those who call themselves the People of God, a people who claim the guidance, the inspiration and the possession of a Holy Spirit. As a story studied for its uniqueness, it comes across less as a spiritual biography of a people and more the spiritual biography of God himself in their regard. It is the narrative of the divine action and self-communication for the purpose of our salvation. Yet there is a more profound dimension. I name this the autobiographical level. For now God is heard as writing his own story in his Word and bringing that into the hearing of his people through the Spirit — so that they can interpret it as God's "first person" involvement with us as Emmanuel. Through the Spirit, believers can appropriate this story as their own: "He loved me and gave himself for me" (Gal 2,20). The divine autobiography in Word and Spirit invites to a redemptive retelling of all our autobiographies to the point where we are released to a new sense of our identity in the light of God: "It has not yet appeared what we shall be but when he appears we shall be like him (1 Jn 3,2).

By sketching these general points on the biblical data as narrative, I am stressing the dynamic personal character of the presentation of God as Spirit, Word and Father. Each of these terms is a point from which the whole story can be told, as each appeals to a different aspect of our human existence. If we are touching on the limits of our existence in finitude, mortality and dread, it is not likely that we will tell the story around the person of the Father who so loved the world as to give his own Son. When we are pierced with the sense of guilt and of the terrible power of evil within and beyond us, it is not inappropriate for the narrative to find its turning point in the person of the Son as the one who most shares our evils through the cross, and through it, opens a way to lasting life. If we are lost in a world of fragmentation or locked in a sense of incapacity and power-lessness, the Holy Spirit becomes the telling point. For he leads to truth, to new freedom, and inspires a new world of relationships to God, Christ and our neighbour.

In contrast to the strict dogmatic order of Father/Son/ Spirit, the New Testament narrative is rather free in its expressions of the autobiography of the God of our salvation. Very evidently, we have, say, in John's Gospel, the Father sending the Son — followed by the Father and the Son sending the Spirit. Yet in other writings, is there not a sense in which the Spirit is first, say, in the formation of creation, in forming God's people, forming Christ as the Son of God in power to the glory of the Father? Moltmann especially goes through these variations of the biblical narrative of the Trinity (see *The Trinity and the Kingdom of God,* SCM, 1981, 74-94).

Still, the point is simple: Spirit, Father and Son are not immediately dogmatic terms but narrative terms designating the *dramatis personae* in the story of human salvation. It is odd that the Spirit, so large a presence in the biblical narrative, became so peripheral in so much theology. The theological system must serve the story, not stop it. It could be that the reality of the Spirit can only be intimated in narrative form, in concrete terms as the Breath of Life sensed in our best and most hopeful stories.

5. The Symbol of the Spirit: Has the Heart Lost the Spirit in the Head?

The trinitarian terms of the narrative of the Gospel are clearly symbols before they are definitions or theological con-cepts. They function as a dynamic whole, these three symbols basic to the Christian experience of God, Father, Son, Holy Breath. The basic symbolism of the Spirit is extended in terms of wind, fire, fountain, dove. By noting the symbolic designation of the divine Mystery, we are alerting ourselves in one more way, to the affective experience of God's being and action. God acts for our conversion to the real promise of life — not to teach us systematic theology or exegesis, even though there must be a place for such worthy disciplines in the divine plan! The self-revelation of God occurs on the level of praxis, in all our living relationships to other, to society, to the world itself. Christian Duquoc in his *Dieu Différent* (Cerf: Paris, 1977) suggests that trinitarian symbolism has a psychological function in promoting Christian conversion. What it works to convert us from is the world of false religion, so powerfully criticised by Marx and Freud. It is a world of infantile imagination (*l'imaginaire*) where narcissism, not self-transcendence holds sway. In more biblical terms, this is, no doubt, the world of idols (projections of self) and demons (unintegrated desire and instinct which end by possessing at the expense of being responsibly possessed). In short, it is the world of infantile omnipotence and social irresponsibility.

It is important in this context to think of the three main terms of trinitarian symbolism functioning together. When they do, they inspire a certain level of conversion. If they are not caught up in a dynamic of affective interrelationship, they can each degenerate into a false type of religious consciousness. For example, "Father" (the most ambiguous of the symbols) unrelated to the real world of the adult "Son" crucified for his brethren, can end in being just a "father-image" psychically manipulated to insure against the pain of growth and love. Similarly, the "Son", detached from the claims and saving will of the "Father" can degenerate as an image: "Son" can end by connoting a "gentle Jesus", even the "Baby Jesus", ignorant of passion, anger, the experience of darkness and the demands of love, and so serving as a model for a regressive "divine childhood". Influenced by such a sentimental sonship or childhood, perhaps the believer is led to hope that he can be spared responsibility and that the God against whom he nestles will make all the bad things simply go away.

In the same way, the symbolism of the Spirit can go bad.

Detached from the interplay of the Father/Son relationship with its focus in the Kingdom and the cross, the inspiration of the Spirit can be invoked to legitimate a wild enthusiasm and even fairly crude self-indulgence — as Paul had to explain to his Corinthians.

But trinitarian symbolism occurs as a healing for such degenerate religious affectivity. It functions to summon the believer from a religion of security and enclosed individuality to a self-giving, other-regarding existence in the service of love. In the Son we find the way of true service of God and neighbour. In the Father, we find the ultimate mystery in which we all belong as "our Father". In the Spirit, we are inspired and supported in the exigencies of a truly Christ-conformed, outgoing love.

Since the Spirit is our special concern here, let me make four points on how Spirit-symbolism functions in the believer's affectivity. I am following Duquoc's line of thought.

1. The Spirit is the energy of a new creation: the presence of the Spirit exorcises any fatal fascination with the past. It opens the community to the "ever-new" of God. There is no return to secure paradise, no safety in law or temple. It is a force for mission into the novelty of history, into an un-manipulable future out of which God comes to meet us. The activity of the Spirit makes believers see that the Father's house is not the hospitality of a familiar earthly home; but, with the security of the past left behind, the future fulfilment where God welcomes us beyond the darkness of the cross. The Spirit acts to overcome the inertia that neither envisages nor desires transformation, and the conversion leading to it. The Spirit opens a gap that only God can fill.

2. The Spirit inspires liberty: not a spirit of slavery but of freedom (Rom 8,12-17), to be free from sin, anxiety, law; to be free with God as Abba; free for the following of Christ. Such a freedom does not negate law, since, as Paul knew, good laws remain as the responsible structuring of just and loving relationships. But the Spirit relativises law. It is not a way of manipulating God. It is not an object of absolute trust. The freedom of the Spirit bends law to the service of life,

and so contests any ideology of absolute conformity. The Sabbath is made for man. . . . Once more we see the Spirit opening a space in human structures that only God can fill. . . .

3. The Spirit is communion (1 Cor 12,4-11; 27-30): In contesting the narcissistic imagination, the Spirit is the revelation of the other not as a threat but as a gift. This does not mean that communion means a fusion into some kind of undifferentiated unity. The union that the Spirit founds is a communion in which otherness, that of the Gentile to the Jew, the male to the female, those gifted in ways other than oneself, is an experience of grace. In such a play of symbolism, the Spirit is a field of relationships in which there is communion in difference. Once more the Spirit is the presence of an openness and space which lets in the fullness of God.

4. The Spirit as an agent of memory: though the force of the future, the Spirit is an agent of faithful recall. He inspires a creative remembering of the real life of the Son in the real world of service and struggle. He inspires the ever dangerous memory of Jesus' solidarity with the outcast, the defeated, the hopeless and the handicapped. He is the divine resistance to any version of the future which would forget the challenge of the past. Though he is the Spirit of resurrection, it is always the resurrection of the crucified; and of those who take up their cross and follow him. Again, we note, the Spirit is the agent of openness, demanding that we make space for the crucified one in our past, the spirit of *anamnesis,* not of amnesia.

In short, the symbolism of the Spirit evokes a sense of space and distinction. Given the traditional language of union associated with the mystery of the Spirit, it might appear brash to suggest that the Spirit is the Spirit of gracious apartness — even to the point of implying that he keeps Father and Son "apart". However, the trinitarian God is no self-sufficient, self-enclosed God. The Trinity is a self-communicating God. For to be God, to be the Absolute, does not mean an absolute unity excluding all distinction. There are the Father and the Son. Certainly a distinction. But even this

Father/Son relationship is not one of total self-sufficiency in a completely symmetrical possession of the other, as though God were only the Father contemplating his perfect self-expression in the Son, who is turned to the Father as his total origin and goal. For the Spirit intervenes as the divine third, the divine "in between". Of course, words fail, but it is worth the theological risk to try to say something like this: the Spirit is not only the common spirit of the Father and the Son; but, as distinct from each of them, he is, in the heart of the Trinity, God's being infinitely more than a self-enclosed symmetrical relationship. The Spirit is God's freedom to be ecstatic, to be infinitely open to the infinite domain of divine freedom, to creation, and indeed, to an infinity of worlds. He is the divine possibility of being, in love, infinitely more than Divine Mind and Divine Word related to one another in reciprocal fulfilment. Is this the reason why, in creation, in history, in Christ, the Spirit is always mysteriously, creatively "there" before he is fully given after the resurrection? As the Spirit of creation and redemption, the Spirit is the divine space and openness of freedom by which God calls what is not-God into being.

Admittedly, such probes are not formal theological statements. They are trying to evoke the play of trinitarian symbolism as it resonates in our affectivity; as it affects the way we feel about God. Still, "the symbol gives rise to thought" (Ricoeur), and thought can go on to probe more objectively the mystery of the Spirit.

6. The Spirit and Inter-Faith Communication: Is "Logos Theology" Enough?

Peter's problem in visiting the house of Cornelius is now transposed, in our day, to include the dimensions of the great religions of the world. Raimundo Panikkar has not been alone in suggesting the elements of what follows here. (R. Panikkar, *The Trinity and the Religious Experience of Man,* Orbis: NY, 1973.) A strong incarnational, Logos-centred theology has enabled Christianity in the past to relate, negatively and positively, to religions of the Word, e.g. Israel and Islam. But the grace of our present encounter with religions is demanding something more, if we are to relate redemptively, in giving and receiving, to religions that have no theology of the Word — e.g. Buddhism and Hinduism. For Buddhism has no "God-talk" at all. It aims to bring about release from the disease of human desire into the fulfilment of *nirvana*: there stillness and silence reign; there no conceptual answer, no questioning even, is to be permitted to disturb the Buddha's smile. Through detachment and negation, wordless enlightenment is reached.

Hinduism, especially Advaitan Hinduism, rejects any dualism in ultimate reality: the empirical, historical, illusory ego is absorbed into the true Self, which is both divine and the source of all self-realisation.

Christianity today needs to activate its resources of trinitarian faith if it is going to pass over redemptively to the other world religions and return to itself enriched. Our dogmatic struggles, our limited missionary experience, have made us too much a "Logos religion". It would seem that we need now a more perichoretic trinitarian approach to the realm of religious experience in the great traditions of the present age. Only such an approach would enable the emergence of a truly global Christianity.

The elements of such an approach are there: i) our traditional theology of the Word, which continues to demand further dialogue with Israel and Islam; ii) The larger context of the Word in the context of mysticism of "Father" religion "whom no man has ever seen" (Jn 1,18). The sense of this ultimate inexpressible mystery is typified in the Buddhist experience. And the language of Christian mystical experience has always approximated to this: "Nothing, nothing, nothing . . . and even on the mountain nothing . . ." (John of the Cross, *Ascent of Mount Carmel*). iii) The Christian meaning of the indwelling Spirit allows for a positive appreciation of the Hindu experience as the mysticism of the Spirit and divine immanence. The language of the Upanishads stresses that the *atman* (self), the *ahman* (I) and the *Brahman* (The Divine) are one. This is a challenge to express the meaning of the Spirit as the depth of our true selfhood where we and God are one, in the reality of love. The one Spirit in two subjects, i.e. in the Father and the Son, becomes the one Spirit of many subjects (e.g. in the Church). The Spirit draws us to the Real Centre. As Gift, he inspires a new identity *intimior intimo meo* (St. Augustine). Now God is not so much the supreme Other, but the deepest self, the deepest way of being self in an ultimate Being-in-Love. Compared to this, all other forms of self-realisation are provisional and illusory. This is the area where the Hindu experience challenges our traditional theology of the Spirit to find new categories and to embark on new ways of exploring the mystery of our One-ness with God.

No doubt, any authentic Christianity will proceed to point out that this "Spirit-self" within us impels the Christian to the embodied social, historical, cosmic self-realisation "in Christ": the inner experience leads to an outer journey. Both of these aspects, the inner and the outward are comprehended within the all-originating and all-attracting mystery of the Father: God ever beyond us as infinite fulfilment is with us (in Christ) and within us (in the Spirit). Still, Christianity's redemptive completion of Hinduism is only possible if such a Christianity has been first enriched by a genuine passing over into the spiritual depths of Hinduism's deep interior mysticism.

For those who would fear the emergence of a superficial syncretism, I would recall the hardiness in which Augustine sought the *vestigia trinitatis* in all creation; the freedom of the medievals in their practice of appropriation; and the "Cornelius problem" of Peter in the early Church (Ac 10). There are precedents. But neither Peter nor Augustine nor Thomas Aquinas had today's opportunity to explore the globally reconciling proportion of trinitarian faith. As always, theology tends to arrive a little out of breath when it comes to catching up with "Holy Breath" of God.

Now we pass on to the final point where most theologies begin.

7. Models of the Spirit: Is the Mystery of the Spirit Greater than the Model?

In theological tradition, it has always been a well-accredited procedure to look for ways of illuminating our understanding of the Trinity through the use of analogy. Since the world issues forth from God, it must contain "traces", *vestigia,* of its divine efficient, final and exemplary cause. And since man is made in the image of God, it is above all human existence which supplies fruitful analogies regarding the being and life of God. Further, since the human spirit, with its special faculties of intellect and will, is the highest perfection of human being, then it is above all in human spiritual activity that we look for terms to disclose, in some analogical way, the ultimate mystery from which we live. In such a context, there arises the Psychological Image. This was elaborated in some half a dozen ways by St. Augustine. It was brought to an impressive systematic precision by Aquinas.

Thomas Aquinas uses the psychological analogy to throw some light on how there can be two processions in God, how there can be relationships within God, and how the divine persons can be conceived of as distinctly subsisting relationships, and so forth. The Holy Spirit is related to the procession of love: God utters himself, and all creation, in the Word; and rejoices in what is so comprehended in love. The Spirit is God's infinite joy in being God, God's unlimited being-in-love.

Now, I would not want to minimise the elegance or usefulness of this basic analogy. It clarifies and co-ordinates so much of the biblical data, especially in regard to the processions of the Son/Word and Spirit and their sequence. Indeed, because this analogy was and is so elegantly systematic, it can work to close our eyes to the full richness of the biblical data, some aspects of which I have indicated in speaking of trinitarian symbolism and narrative. One could be pardoned for suspecting that the psychological analogy certainly puts the divine persons "into" God, but can't quite manage to get them out again in the economy of salvation, especially the Holy Spirit. For the personal presence of the Spirit in the history of salvation was often dogged with the designation of being merely "appropriated". Thus so much of the realism of the biblical witness was undercut.

Rahner's insistence on the identity of the economic and

the immanent Trinity did a lot to remind theology that our analogies are meant to serve the given mystery, the *Datum,* the *Donum,* not to encapsulate it. I think, too, that Lonergan's attempt to transpose the psychological analogy from a metaphysical faculty analysis to a more contemporary intentionality analysis has brought more experiential and critical awareness into this traditional theological procedure. It enables one to see how the experience of our own individual and communal self-realisation in meaning and value can re-express in contemporary terms the mystery of the divine selfhood as a dynamic of self-realisation: the divine self-constitution in infinite meaning and infinite value is the redemptive ground of all human search for common meaning and for self-transcending values, as the condition for the emergence of the one global humanity.

Further, by locating the analogy in human consciousness rather than in Aristotelian metaphysical psychology, we are moving toward a more creative way of expressing the reality of the Spirit. In the old metaphysical scheme, the love of the Spirit had to follow the Word of Truth: *nil amatum nisi praecognitum.* In the contemporary analysis of praxis-oriented consciousness there are experiences that justify a reversal of this sequence as *nil cognitum nisi praeamatum;* i.e. unless we have surrendered ourselves to something, committed ourselves to it, loved it, we cannot know it as our truth. Our best words bring to expression what we love. A trinitarian analogy arising out of this kind of experience has two advantages: i) it enables us to respect a certain primacy of the Spirit in regard to the Word, e.g. in the Lukan pneumatology; and ii) it provides a possible move for the breaking of the deadlock with the Eastern Churches over the *Filioque.* Indeed, it suggests that the Son/Word proceeds from the Father *Spirituque,* in a way that would provoke a new context for dogmatic discussion.

Then again, there is another kind of psychological analogy, drawn from intersubjectivity. This too has a noble theological pedigree, though it often gets scant systematic attention because of the danger of tritheism. But it could be insisted that this was the original analogy: "Let us make man in our image and likeness . . . male and female he created them" (Gn 1,27f). The archetypal human community imaged the reality of God. Modern theology has taken up this original lead by using the resources of personalist philosophies and community categories. Thus, we have H. Muehlen presenting the Spirit as the "We-Act", the communal acting "We" of the Father and the Son, communicated to the Church. So that the Spirit is always the One Person in the many. God's subsisting unitive love.

True, traditional trinitarian theology has often pounced disapprovingly on such community analogies. But in the modern context more aware of the use of models, and of their limitation and complementarity, it is not seen as a destructive relativism to admit a number of models to explore the Mystery (or of any reality). Not all maps of Australia begin from the same point. Nor are they concerned to highlight the same features. If any map tried to represent everything all at once, e.g. the demographic distribution, geological strata, industrial concentration, fauna and flora, waterways, climate, communication systems and political alignments, it would be useless. Now a model is a kind of map. And it is an aspect of theological adoration to permit the fulness of the mystery to be explored in a number of ways. . . . The Spirit both invites and escapes our use of models and analogies.

So, seven ways to approach the Mystery of the Spirit. I would hope "seven gifts"; different ways of saying "Come, Holy Spirit".

1. See an excellent article, "The Person of the Holy Spirit" in *The Holy Spirit and Power. The Catholic Charismatic Renewal*, K. McDonnel, OSB (ed.), New York: Doubleday, 11-32.

8

Who belongs to the Church?

"WHO needs the Church?", "Why am I a Catholic?", "Why do you stay in?" are questions prevalent enough in the conversations and writings of Christians and Catholics today. But a hurried answer to any of these delays facing up to one more question which is the profound one. "Who really belongs to the Church?"

All kinds of options are being painfully and confusedly lived out which receive no special help from a theology content to discourse endlessly on "Models of the Church". Here especially "model talk" has become an easy escape from real issues. Of course, we are often told that the Church is no longer to be understood as a "thing", "out there" apart from us, for now *we* are the Church, indeed, the People of God. Well, that doesn't necessarily bring much light to the question we are considering. It succeeds only in making us experience this query as something more intimate and more urgent. If we are really to lay claim to this new reality that is being offered, are not we the ones to determine our manner of belonging to the Church? Do we belong, then, on our own terms?

Yet, we are belonging to *something;* we are standing with and for *something* intrinsically connected with our hope for the fullness of life for all humanity. Are our criteria for belonging to such a reality purely subjective? Who really belongs, and how do they belong?

Take, for instance, the lamentable situation that obtains at the moment regarding the implementation of the Third Rite of Reconciliation. This whole sorry discussion conceals at root the question, "Who deserves to participate in the sacramental ministry of the Church?" All those urgent questions about baptism, the nature of marriage, common ministries and intercommunion are clearly connected with the basic question of who belongs in the Church and how they belong.

Since such a question is intrinsically connected with the identity of the Church, it is very urgent. If we concede that the Church has a right to exist, it has a right to form its identity and to defend it. This entails the necessity of drawing boundaries, and of discriminating between what it is and what it is not. Here we are concerned with the challenges the Church faces in this process of discrimination and self-determination.

A. Why a New Experience of the Question?

First of all, the old way of belonging to the Church has broken down. Such a pattern of belonging was forged through the experience of the Counter-Reformation, articulated with Scholastic precision, with all that special emphasis on the acceptance of doctrines and sacramental practice which were made into issues by the reformers.

Then, again, a tightknit Catholicism was underpinned by the shared vision and sensibilities of a Christendom which has been formed by the Church of the Middle Ages. Only now do we realise how completely Catholic and Protestant still shared a world, despite the doctrinal and political differences.

For us Catholics the juridical determination of how we belonged to the Church was rather clear-cut. The Church was a "perfect society" sufficient to itself for the attainment of its supernatural end, confident in forming its own laws and norms, capable of determining the right expression of the faith and of supervising the licit and valid administration of the sacraments. Church members had rights and duties unless some *obex* intervened. Criteria for heresy were stated clearly as when a Church-taught doctrine was denied, whilst those who would reject the authority of the Church, especially papal authority, were duly termed "schismatic" (Canon 1325).

Most obviously there was a great assurance in this juridic determination of who belonged or not to the Church. The profound and beautiful theology of *Mystici Corporis* showed how the Church was infinitely more than its juridical institution; but the one was co-extensive with the other: the "Mystical" and Juridical" body were quite correlative. Those outside the visible communion of the Catholic Church were not disowned even if their Church-status was not recognised. Seemingly only as individuals could they be related to the Mystical Body of the Redeemer "by a certain unconscious desire" (inscio quodam desiderio ac voto) par. 101.

In the present world of immense and dramatic changes, such a manner of viewing Church membership has become all but impossible. Profound cultural changes have undermined the apparently stolidly visible structure of the past. This is most obvious in regard to marriage and its Christian celebration. Canonical practice has been forced to consider so many new questions in its interpretation of indissolubility, to take but one example.

Culture as a whole has been rapidly secularised and placed under the direction of "science" and its attendant totalitarian ideologies. Pluralism in our interpretation of life and the world we so precariously share, is an inescapable fact. The Church is no longer able to articulate the faith with the Latin precision of Scholastic philosophy. Vatican II has shown the Church thinking with a more biblical style, in more personalist categories, with more existential concerns. Missionary theory calls her to be involved in a variety of cultures, and differing socio-economic structures are demanding that the Church be present in different ways. Those promoting or resisting such developments make contestation a feature of the "tempest-tossed" life of the People of God. The result is that the institutional structures are swamped with such a variety of urgent issues that the juridic system is no longer able to hold and function as before. The "moral cases" of individual Christian conscience are suddenly replaced by the dramatic issues of human survival, a world system of justice, peace, the arms race, the continuing threat of thermo-nuclear war, the destruction of the environment, exploitation and the oppression of whole races of peoples. The "moral cases" of micro-morality are all but forgotten in the presence of the macro-moral issues that demand immediate attention. How do we judge who is most Christian, most Catholic? The one who follows *Humanae Vitae* or the one who takes *Populorum Progressio* as Gospel-truth?

It should be clear that the old system of determining belonging is no longer adequate for the world has so changed. But part of the reason for the breakdown of the clear juridical system is the express teaching of Vatican II. The Council no longer identifies the Mystical Body purely and simply with the Catholic Church, or (adds Congar, significantly) even "with the Church of Christ",[1] for "this Church subsists in the Catholic Church though many elements of sanctification and truth are found outside her visible structures'. (*Lumen Gentium,* par. 8; and also the *Decree on Ecumenism,* par. 4; *Declaration on Religious Freedom,* par. 1).

The tendency to excommunicate those departing from orthodoxy now seems to be replaced with a discerning desire to incorporate. Thus, the question of how we belong to the Church is being felt in a new way. With this perhaps odd notion of "subsistence", the Mystery of the Church seems to be conceived of as a great field of life-giving energy, more or less concentrated at particular points or around particular structures. In the light of such an understanding of the Church, Congar concedes that as the past unconditional interpretation passes, "the result is a loss of a certain simplicity in matters of faith".[2] Who would disagree?

This loss of a "certain simplicity" is certainly felt in the question of how we belong to the Church. A new reality is being forced onto our consideration. This provides an occasion for theology to be more closely instructed by a *Sociology of Religious Belonging* (Carrier *et al.*)[3]

The former unconditional objectivity is in no small measure at the mercy of the "subjective turn" so characteristic of our era. Any objective statement is apprehended as the outcome of a largely subjective process which constructs the social reality of human life. The complicated processes of hermeneutics seems almost to lead us to the point where we have all but lost our grip on the *given,* understood as objectively valid data. However, to acknowledge the complexity of the passage from the subject to the object is also to be given an opportunity to become more aware of the intimacy and delicacy of the mysteries which involve us.

There is a practical outcome to all this. In the midst of dramatic issues which so structure our experience of the world, when these attain to a special immediacy through the mass-media, we are clearly a long way from any easy determination of heresy and schism. We are being involved in a new way of experiencing the human reality of belonging to the Church. Because we are related in such a range of rapid and multi-media communication, knowledge seems to have become far more obviously a process in which the word is but one aspect. Surely the Church is under the necessity of protecting its identity; but the old ways of analysing propositions as criteria of orthodoxy are surely inadequate.

Then, too, in a secular society characterised by pragmatism, doctrinal systems are apprehended as relative to ostensible results. Pragmatically formed minds see all thought and reflection as leading to a transformation of the world. Similarly, faith and the whole reality of the Church are evaluated in their capacity to bring a more human quality into life. Such an attitude can undoubtedly threaten the Christian message in its true originality and independence. But, at best, a healthy pragmatism can remind us of the genuine concern of Gospel, to bring salvation to mankind: Christ came into the world to save sinners — not to teach them theology, not even to catechise them regarding true doctrine. Theology and catechesis are moments in the greater process of the transformation of humankind by the Spirit of God. Whatever the case given the concentrated pragmatism of our technological times, can the Church in her concern for her own unity and integrity afford to place such emphasis on the objectively doctrinal expression of faith? Difficult though it is to express, are we not all feeling that the most searching principle of discrimination is now in the realm of practice. There is at least slogan value in saying that orthopraxy now replaces orthodoxy: right action replaces right confession of the faith as the important element.

If we can see something in this, clearly we are beginning to experience the manner of belonging to the Church in a different fashion. And, indeed, let us concede that questions still remain: who is really doing the "right thing"? At least "right belief" allowed for a variety of action. The danger is apparent: a new self-justifying *orthodoxy,* in the name of orthopraxy, replacing the older, more genuinely catholic orthodoxy. However, there are dangers in everything, and, I think, the point remains that we are experiencing new imperatives in the meaning of Christian existence today.

But there is an even larger consideration. I can refer to it best by appealing to a work like Walbert Buhlmann's *"The Coming of the Third Church".*[4] The Church is ceasing to be so decisively European. Already the majority of Catholics belong to the Third World of Africa, South America, Asia and Oceania. By 2000 we can predict that nearly 75% of Catholics will be found in the poorer, more youthful, indeed more "religious" countries beyond Europe. As the Church begins to understand herself more through dialogue with these populous, economically deprived, spiritually rich regions, and less through the conversation hitherto monopolised by now ageing European agnostics, a new sense of identity will surely emerge.

It is to be expected that the question of belonging to the Church will be posed in an increasingly new fashion. As the Church expands and develops in these comparatively less clericalised societies and given the fewness of priests, traditional doctrinal and sacramental modes of belonging will be subsumed into a new vision and sense of the reality of belonging.

These considerations lead us to the next series of reflections: from the "Why?" of the new experience of the question, we go to the "How?"

B. How the Question of Belonging to the Church Is Being Experienced in a New Way:

Let us straightaway mention that the "Unconditional" ways of belonging to the Church articulated in the older theology were never quite as cut and dried as they may have appeared. For theology, always massively influenced by St. Augustine, was aware of his oft-repeated statement: "Many of those who are thought to be on the outside will be found to be within; and many who are apparently within, will be found to be excluded". Then, too, baptism of desire and blood are notably flexible concepts. The place (if not the rights) of conscience was always theoretically recognised within the Catholic system (though Newman was a long time coming). The ancient dictum, "Extra ecclesiam, nulla salus" was interpreted in an increasingly benign fashion.

The New Testament itself continued to witness to the many ways of belonging to Christ in the "many mansions" of the Father's house; there were those who but occasionally heeded the word of Jesus and the disciples (to bring forth differing percentages of yield). Some sought aid from him in sickness and guilt; there were more less secret disciples like Nicodemus — all these having a place before and perhaps after the fully-fledged Pentecostal community. Even this, striving though it did for complete unity in Christ, lived with differing developments of ministry, differing personal influences, differing theologies . . .

All the time in the life of Christian communities practical solutions were being found. In the living experiences of the laity in places like Australia, a tacit ecumenism of respect worked in many social occasions. A wider sense of the Church was the secret of such communities long before it became a theological imperative. All those sacraments of common humanity, "decency", if you like, were a striking and palpable reality in moments of tragedy (e.g. war), in concerns of common interest (e.g. trade unions), or in moments of simple enjoyment (e.g. sport). This type of experience is worth bringing to mind since it has been so mute for so long. Perhaps people living all their Christian history in a

102

pluralist society have in fact discovered a sense of the Church but recently understood in Europe.

Nonetheless, the principle of drawing boundaries is to be accepted if the Church is to have an identity. Von Balthasar reminds us that the line was indeed drawn, "and not without pain and struggle".[5] In the Old Testament the criteria for belonging to the Chosen people were unproblematical. But in the New Testament, complexities were of the nature of the case: Paul, in the authority of Christ, excludes sinners from the community (1 Cor 5,4; 1 Tim 1,20); the principle of "binding and loosing" was applied (Mt 18, 17ff). In 2 Thes 2,14f, the sinner though reproved, is still avoided by the community. Those causing divisions and scandals were always a matter of intense concern (for Paul: 1 Cor 8,7; Rom 16,17; Tt 3,10; for John: especially 1 Jn 2,19f; 2 Jn 9f). Then there is the very intriguing Jude 1,21ff.

So there is plenty of data that the Church of the New Testament experienced the problems of boundaries. The overall impression is that they were felt and faced on the level of the local community rather than in the context of the "Church Universal" as we have tended to experience them. As the Church after Vatican II moves back to a consciousness of the "local Church", and within this to the question of "Basic Christian Communities", the consequence is, naturally, that we are experiencing the old questions in a way that is new to us, and, indeed, in a way that requires personal attitudes and decisions on our part. The problems of Pope or bishop discerning "heresy" or "schism" are now very often our own. Do certain people or groups really belong to us in the one faith — or are they just using us for their own purposes? Questions like this cannot be indefinitely shelved.

But, to stress the point again, we cannot so easily use the "doctrinal test", given the unresolved pluralism of theologies. Undoubtedly, we are in a time of primary reflection in theology where the basic questions so long taken for granted are being posed and explored. We are experiencing Vatican II's principle of the "hierarchy of truths" in a practical way. For example, theology must give so much time to showing how our theological speech is valid *in some way*. The issues of angels, indulgences, practical piety and so forth are seldom treated. We must, then, really ask whether or not we are in a time of waiting since we know all too well that there are severe limitations on our capacity to experience and express the whole truth. Is it right to speak and act with a certain patience and tolerance of confusion rather than to draw the lines too urgently and too tightly, with the danger of forcing "weaker (or stronger?) brethren" into rigid positions whereby they must define themselves as outside the Church?

The dilemma is so familiar: is the traditional expression of faith the pre-eminent value, or fellowship with those who are at least asking the right questions and searching for a solution? Will time solve this kind of problem?

We can so easily become a little neurotic about clear lines of division especially when a certain ambiguity seems to be necessarily involved in our present situation. If the Church is involved in dialogue with non-Catholics, non-Christians, Marxists, Humanists or whomever else, the conditions of dialogue need to be accepted. A monologue composed of slogans shouted across barricades is far more clear than candid friendly conversation. We may work with a kind of "picture book" theology which has clear labels for Church and world, sacred and secular, Christian and humanist and so on. But the world is not like that anymore . . . if it ever was "once upon a time . . ." We Christians are so often on both sides of the dialogue . . . or, more likely the dialogue happens mainly within ourselves.

Or you may prefer to approach the matter more technically by using, say, something like Lonergan's model of the conversion process.[6] He isolates intellectual, moral and religious aspects of conversion (you could add Christian, ecclesial and psychological). I would just mention that no one can grapple with the whole dynamism of conversion as one simple event. In our times when our experience of the transcendent is being so re-ordered, we need to be rather humble, first of all, in the realisation that no one of us is totally converted to the fullness of Christ. You see, we might experience this call to conversion primarily as an imperative to be far more objective, broad-minded and hard headed in an effort to overcome what is narrow and parochial in our attitudes, and to accept truth where it can be found. So faith tries to meet and learn from modern science, psychology, sociology, anthropology and so forth.

Then again, it is another type of event when our conscience stirs us to develop a commitment to new types of values that we have hitherto neglected. If the former type of conversion is more intellectual, this is moral in character: we are impelled to a new awareness of racism, economic oppression, ecology and the environment, the fragility of peace and the dreadful inventiveness of the international arms pedlars. Such issues are almost of their nature all-absorbing, and tend to form us into a special world of ultimate concern within which we enunciate the relevance of the Gospel.

As a final example, there is the religious possibility of conversion. Perhaps it occurs to those who do their share of the world's work when they experience frustration, selfishness and betrayal, and are all but destroyed by the power of evil. They feel impelled to somehow resolve those agonising questions like: Is there really hope for us? . . . Is there someone to forgive us? . . . To whom, finally, are we really responsible? Is there one to save our souls . . . to save the worth of everything we have put ourselves into and poured ourselves out for?

We could give other examples of other levels of conversion. The point is that if they are all part of the dynamism of our conversion to the risen humanity of Christ, they each tend to structure the criteria for belonging to the Christian community in a different way, one more philosophical, another more practical, a third more contemplative. . . .

Congar, as he tries to overcome an unusual despondence about the collapse of the former criteria, comes up with a practical suggestion. He suggests that we should consider the establishment of a kind of "Threshold Church", a kind of modern Church of the Cathechumens, a way of belonging suitable to all those (he has youth very much in mind) who do not feel themselves capable of full incorporation into the complete sacramental visibility of the Church.[7]

I am sure there is something in this. How many "leave

the Church" before they have had a chance to join it? Should we force them prematurely to declare themselves? Above all, should we put them in a position where they are morally forced either to "receive" or "refuse" the sacraments? In the present situation characterised by confusion and ambiguity, I do not think so. But neither can we let them drift away, unheard, unwelcomed, uncared for.

We need to find space where these problems can be sorted out. It is hardly possible or desirable to retire into agnostic exclusivism, a more intellectually justified ghetto. But the present situation will not do: holding the line and allowing for an increasing number of special cases . . . which become *so very numerous.* (For example, think once more on the indissolubility of Christian marriage and the growing number of special cases).

A special regime allowing for this threshold status allows for a welcoming space where problems can be sorted out, and, perhaps, where all of us might learn more. This gives a very concrete expression to our adoration of the Spirit at work in the world. The Spirit does not lead us all, all at once, to discern the full meaning of the Word of God as it is manifest in Christ. The tradition remains as the source of Christian identity; but it is a tradition activated only in the context of communication in the present. The notion of tradition may not be used to lessen the possibility of the great human aspirations making their presence felt in the heart of the Church, in the urgency of the present moment. Some associated with the Church in this way may not be free to "receive the sacraments". Perhaps it is sufficient to be a sacrament of a more compassionate humanity in the name of Christ.

The question of boundaries is occurring in a more relational way, within the untidiness and exuberance of a confused situation, where inherited cultures are in disarray and so many are awakening to a new sense of our oneness on this globe.

This raises the question of the kind of leadership needed in the Church where the boundaries of belonging are being redrawn. Leaders in the Church of today will need to be able to communicate with all sections of the Church. The leadership of mediation is most needed, an ability to span the breadth between the limits of doctrine and action, sacrament and reality, contemplation and involvement. How are such leaders to be found? How is their sphere of action to be defined?

It is not fanciful to suppose that such leaders should be taken up in improvising celebrations of belonging since the codification of the variety of excommunication hardly suits our present needs. In this context, the notion of some kind of "provisional sacraments" will have to be explored. For the many unable or unprepared to communicate in the traditional sacraments (as they will continue to be celebrated in the Church) who continue to understand their lives "in light of Christ", some ritual of belonging needs to be devised. Such would embody a shared unity in the Spirit even though this can only anticipate full incorporation into the Church. It would face people towards the fullness of Church-faith without demanding of them an impossible level of commitment. It is hard to see how anyone is helped by an indiscriminate celebration of the Eucharist. It is, after all, the most intense point of communal belonging as Catholics (or Christians, as the case may be). So many of the practical questions on intercommunion seem to imply an excessively sacramental view of belonging to the Church. Might we not be better served in trying to re-activate the symbolism of the *Agape* or fraternal meal? Rather than refuse or demand communion, we might better invite communication in our degrees of faith only at that level of intensity that can be appreciated as real and genuine.

I am sure that the sorry history of the Third Rite of Reconciliation might yet teach us something. Certainly, behind the strained interpretations, the conflicting statements, the unpredictable restrictions, there is a view on what belonging to the Church means. On the other hand, "Rite III" might be the most pertinent sacramental formula of our time. It creates a friendly and compassionate space and invites to a further and more personal participation in the Mystery of Christ. And, situated so obviously in the context of community, where reconciliation and the need for it can be keenly experienced, it has a certain obviously *real content* for those who are looking for the saving reality of Christ.

How do we belong to the Church today? In raising the question, I hope I have contributed to an appreciation of the complexity of the issues, to an awareness of the limits and the promise of the present situation.

Let me conclude with two remarks:

First, this type of reflection is an expression of the basic paradox involved in being the Church. For to be the Church is to be sacrament of Universal Redeeming Love. The Church dare not risk communicating anything but the genuine content of this unique message — but it is a message *for everyone,* and a reality open to every human being. The problem arises when the "uniqueness" and the "for everyone" get confused, the one swallowing up the other. Of what value is the message of God's universal Love if it is kept as a perfectly orthodox secret within the confines of the Church? What use is the Church if it is just vaguely and generally "for everyone"?

Secondly, the real terms of this topic concerning belonging to the Church are hidden in the autobiographies of each one of us. How has the Church claimed us as her own? Why are we claiming this Church as ours? How has the Church been so patient with our poor Christianity? How have we not been scandalised by the lack of love?

The question today is complex and urgent. But, in different forms, the answer is hidden in the hearts of those for whom Christ is still the way to abundant life.

1. Y. Congar, "What belonging to the Church has come to mean", *Communio* IV (1977) 146-160.
2. *op. cit.,* 152.
3. Herve Carrier, *The Sociology of Religious Belonging* (Herder and Herder, 1963). Of considerable value, too, is Graham M. S. Dann, "Religious Belonging in a Changing Catholic Church". *Soc. Analysis* 37 (1976), 283-297. Oddly, he makes no reference to Carrier.
4. (St. Paul Publications, Slough, 1976).
5. H. Urs von Balthasar, "The Boundary Line" in *Elucidations* (SPCK 1975) 179-191.
6. *Method in Theology* (DLT, 1973) 267-270, *et passim.*
7. Congar, *op. cit.,* 158ff.

9

The world Church

A RESPECTED colleague was recently giving a talk to our faculty in Melbourne. His topic was Basic Christian Communities. He spoke with great enthusiasm out of his recent experiences during a study tour which took him to many centres in Latin America. He stressed that these basic communities were embodying the commitment of Christian faith in a way that made it truly creative and challenging in the oppressive situations which prevailed. They were a paradigm of the Church of the future.

Of course, I found myself carried along and inspired by what was being said. There was an obvious truth here: the conscientised communities of South America, the Christian ashrams of India, the cell groups in a revitalised modern parish, a variety of African experiments in living the Gospel in the terms of village and tribal life, these all seemed to have something in common. In terms of the Church, too, "small is beautiful". It was that kind of beauty that would last into the future.

But as I heard my colleague's account, there was something in me that resisted. Were these small basic communities the whole truth of the Church? Eventually, I was able to put my question to the speaker in more concrete terms. I said something like this: "You were born in Germany. You belong to an international religious order. You did your doctoral studies in the United States. You've taught for years in the Philippines, and now you run an institute in Italy. You have lived for periods of time in probably half a dozen other countries. At this moment you are back with us here in

Australia after your visit to South America . . . and you have just told us that these small communities are the future shape of the Church. But what you most represent in your own life and work is the emergence of a world Church. Even as you talk about the situation in Latin America to us here in Melbourne this evening, what you are most representing is a global dimension of the Church: different cultures, different patterns of religious experience, different human struggles meet in a richness of communication never possible before. Aren't you forgetting the most obvious feature of the future Church?"

Discussion followed! And as we discussed, the outline of the paradox began to be clear. Small is beautiful because the large, the universal, the *Catholic* thing allows it to be so: the vast, global, catholic dimension of Church-life lived from the distinctive beauty of small groups. The global and the local interpenetrate.

In such a context, the recent phenomenon of travelling Popes is a theological event. If there was a time when "all roads led to Rome", now seems to be the time when Rome comes to kiss the ground in the different regions of the globe. On a lesser scale, the visit of Cardinal Arns of Brazil to a youth festival in Australia, and the recent visit of Dom Helder Camara, infused the local Catholic consciousness with a wider compassion for the world and the Church beyond us.

The Church has to be catholic to serve a new kind of globalism. Positively, a global sense of humanity is necessary if we are to profit from the interchange of skills, art, science, wisdom, human and natural resources now made possible at this stage of history. To speak more negatively, only such a sense of global humanity can prevent us from some form of ecological or military self-destruction. In this case, it is not a high ideal but the condition for any human future. The emerging World Church is in a unique position to serve the world at this decisive moment in history.

Writers such as Walbert Buhlmann, in his recent *Weltkirche* (Styria: Graz, 1984) and the better known *The Coming of the Third Church* (St Paul Publications: Slough,

1976) are stressing the vast shifts in the global character of the Church. As we move to the third millennium in the life of the Church there is good reason for thinking of this as the era of the Church of the South. The first thousand years of Christianity saw most of vitality flowing from the East. The second thousand years, with the conversion of Europe, the high culture of the Middle Ages, the expansion of missionary activity made possible by colonialism, was demonstrably the millennium of the West. But now it would seem that the South is coming into its own.

At least demographically. Take the Catholic Church for example. By the year 2000, seventy per cent of Catholics will be in Africa, Latin America, Oceania and parts of Asia. This massive shift in the distribution of Church membership has occurred in this century: in 1900, two-thirds of Catholics were in Europe/North America. Now the proportion is reversed.

The significance of this in the self-understanding of Catholic Christianity can hardly be imagined. The present two-thirds of Catholics are to be found in very young populations, in contrast to the increasingly geriatric character of the North. The cultures are exuberantly religious compared with the secular and agnostic tone of Europe. These regions are also economically poor and politically unstable. Racially, they are non-white, or at least mixed. And the Christian faith in these parts is still in contact with cultures even older than the classic European culture.

This demographic shift has given rise to a shift in Christian self-understanding. Pastoral policy is declared as an "option for the poor". Theology, so long accustomed to refute the savants of the Enlightenment, now finds little point in dialoguing with ageing European agnostics. It prefers to explore the sense of Christian faith by listening to, and speaking for, the "unpersons", the poor, those whom the march of mainly European history has left behind.

Inculturation is the key word for another option. The prevalent, usually unnoticed, inculturation of Christian faith into that complex of cultures making up modern Europe, is now being expressly extended into dozens of other cultures in Africa, Asia and the Pacific region.

On a similar scale, the minor ecumenism tentatively arrived at by Orthodox, Catholic and Protestant, is now finding a more salutary context. It is the interfaith dialogue taking place amongst Christians, Hindus, Buddhists and Muslims in a way that was never before possible.

To enable new global forms of Christianity to emerge and thrive, the Western Church will have to go through a time of self-dispossession. There are precedents; principally that of the one who "emptied himself and took the form of a servant (Phil 2, 7). The demands of this new global form of the Church inspire a special kind of dread. After all, it is a question of the Western Church dying into a radically different future. Faith is called upon to expand far beyond the proportions of the limited experience of history up to the present. But there is a direction. This is suggested by such basic Christian doctrines as the Resurrection, the Trinity and Grace. Each of these can stimulate an expansion of Christian consciousness to more global proportions.

Take the Resurrection of the Crucified Jesus. His rising from the dead lifts him out of a particular historical existence, to take him beyond the restrictions of time and place. Christian faith implies an entry into this "risen" mode of life. This is meant to make a difference in the way we perceive ourselves and our world. It is meant to inspire a new quality of consciousness. Could this be described as the readiness to stretch beyond one's particular national or cultural existence in a greater openness to the whole of redeemed humanity? To be a Christian today might well demand the capacity to be open to the whole Christ, to pass over in compassion to what was previously alien, to return to where life places us as a brother or sister to every human being, as a citizen of the world.

Belief in the Trinity, too, suggests its own form of planetary consciousness. Up to the present, Christianity has been very much a "Word" religion. This includes the biblical "word of God", of course. But this was quickly related to the Logos-Word of the Greek philosophical tradition. A strong intellectualist culture provided the terms in which early Christian doctrines were formulated. The accent was on orthodox belief, right understanding, and the historical revelation of God in Jesus Christ. Then, in conflict with other religions of the Word, Israel and Islam, Christianity was further formulated in terms of Word. No doubt, this emphasis will remain as the conflicts of the past yield to a more friendly exchange of words, as the *Logos* opens into *dialogos*. (For this point, see Raimundo Panikkar, *The Trinity and The Religious Experience of Man,* New York: Orbis, 1973).

In the present era, however, Christianity is encountering religions which were never so word-centred. Hindu religious experience turns on a transcendent reality into which our illusory transient selves somehow merge. Present individuality is unreal compared to the Real Self awaiting the purified. There what is truly self and truly divine are one. Christian faith can enter into a deeper relationship to such a religious world by deepening its own appreciation of the role of the Holy Spirit. The Spirit is the indwelling God, a force for self-realisation in Christ, impelling believers to a final identity, beyond the fragmented and illusory self-definitions of our mundane existence. In short, the doctrine and experience of the Holy Spirit, "the third divine person" of the Trinity, has become a way of entering into the religious world of Hinduism.

In somewhat the same way, the person of "The Father" in the Christian Trinity invites the followers of Christ to a new appreciation of the Buddhist religious experience. The Buddhist expression of the transcendent is marked by silence, not only of answers, but also of questions. The particular and the finite can never contain the fullness of truth and reality. For the Christian, too, "God dwells in inaccessible light" (1 Tim 6, 16) and "God no man has ever seen" (Jn 1, 18). The origin and end is beyond human comprehension. It is the silence from which the Word proceeds, and to which it returns. It is the depth from which the Holy Breath (Spirit) takes its rise, and to which it leads. Buddhists do not speak of "God". Perhaps their not-speaking is more alert to the character of the ultimate than much of our Christian speech.

Whatever the case, the Christian adoration of "The Father" as the first divine person of the Trinity is a way of sounding, in a constructive way, the depths of the Buddhist experience.

It seems to me that the Christian doctrine of the Trinity has been something of a "sleeper" until this era of interfaith communication. It is showing its full vitality as Christian faith attempts to expand into more planetary proportions.

Another classic Christian doctrine is that of Grace. It, too, is inherently capable of global or planetary expansion. "Grace" is Christian shorthand for the unrestricted character of God's self-giving, as love, as mercy, as our ultimate life. Because it is an unrestricted gift, we should not be surprised if it were as large as life, and capable of provoking a more generous openness to both what God is and what we, human beings on this planet, are or can be together. So it is interesting as we consider the global distribution of the Church, how different regions are tending to experience the gracious self-giving of God in different ways. A loving God is not unaware of the human condition.

Some theologians (Buhlmann and others) speak of the Western experience of grace as a mystery of *salvation* (mysterium salutis). Salvation implies a healing, making whole, a rescue from the wreck. This may well be the clue to the positive character of the Western experience, especially today. For it tends to be concerned with a holistic appreciation of human life in which science and art, male and female, the psychological and the political, the secular and the religious can be pursued as one comprehensive truth. It looks to arrive at a point where the whole of scientifically established reality can yield to a higher transformation, where everything finally comes together, in Christ, in the new form of humanity. Here the holy one tends to be the *philosophos,* the "lover of wisdom". Matthew's Gospel may well be the preferred account of the meaning of faith.

In contrast, the Latin American experience of the grace of Christ is one of *liberation* (mysterium liberationis). God's self-giving accords with the history of this vast complex of cultures and nations, as a force for freedom, in their struggle to break out of political, economic and cultural forms of oppression. Here the holy one is the prophet, and it will not be surprising if he is reading the Gospel according to Mark.

The Asian experience of grace is best expressed in terms of *revelation* (mysterium revelationis). This is the region where the meeting of the great religions of the world is a living experience. In such deeply religious cultures, the divine or the transcendent seems to be "given" as a way or a revealed truth more broadly and intensely than in other cultures. Here the holy one is especially the mystic, and John's Gospel is most read.

In its own manner, the African experience of grace is one of *incarnation* (mysterium incarnationis). African cultures appear to be those most expressive of the exuberant liturgy of life; and where that life is led both with a wonderful spontaneity and corporate sense. Buhlmann is of the opinion that Africans are not such speculative spirits . . . "nicht so sehr speculative Geister und Gruebler" (in contrast with the Teutons, I presume), but more the intuitive artists of life . . . "vielmehr intuitive Lebenskuenstler" (*Weltkiche,* pg. 52). Here, no doubt, the dancer is the holy one, and the joy and openness of Luke's Gospel is the favourite reading.

In the emerging World Church, might we not anticipate great, even if unsettling, meetings amongst these philosophers, prophets, mystics and artists as they share their distinctive experience.

Where is Australia in all this? A few years ago, when I first saw Buhlmann's *The Coming of the Third Church,* I was struck by the cover design. Three continents, Africa, South America and Australia were sketched. So I looked for Australia in the contents. Alas, despite four hundred pages on the shape of the Church to come, Australia did not rate a mention even in the index (though I noticed, under *A,* that everything from abortion to Idi Amin did!) A little symbol perhaps. At least it leaves us with a healthy irony about how others might see us.

But, of course, that is not the point. If we think and pray in a manner large enough to receive the global reality of the

Church as it is emerging, our mediating role in such a world Church may not be inconsiderable.

Somewhere in the world of faith, the wind has changed, and the tide is on the turn, and the Spirit is expanding horizons to allow the earth to be seen as a whole world as never before.

10

Catholic identity:
A theological approach

I BELIEVE the following quotation from George Santayana in *Reason and Religion* (80 years ago he wrote this), makes a valuable point as we approach our subject, Catholic identity. He says, "any attempt to speak without speaking a particular language is not more hopeless than the attempt to have a religion that shall be no religion in particular. Thus, any living and healthy religion has a marked idiosyncrasy. Its power consists in its special and surprising message and in the bias which that revelation gives to life. The vistas it opens up and the mysteries it propounds are another world to live in; and another world to live, whether we expect ever to pass wholly over into it or not, is what we mean by having a religion". (Quoted by C. Geertz, in art. referred to in chapter 3).

Hidden enigmatically in the word *Catholic* are the overtones of its original meaning, namely "universal", "total", "open to all" and the "whole". But still it remains a universality, earthed and embodied. It is placed in history, peopled by generations of men and women with names, living and dying at datable times and in particular places.

It is universal because it is particular. Following the lead expressed in Santayana's words, "being-Catholic" is a particular language for naming oneself, one's community of faith, for praying and celebrating, for asking pardon, for expressing common beliefs; a particular language now austerely ecclesiastical in dogmatic definition, now luxuriantly imaginative in art, liturgy, mysticism—a mother tongue, if you like, in which we

117

express the story of infinite love most tellingly. Thereby we can express who we are in the terms of our faith; and indeed who others are, whether they be near or far.

In the course of this rather personal reflection, I am presuming the Catholic faith is a living and healthy religion; indeed, I experience it as such — disconcertingly so. I will try to "highlight the marked idiosyncrasy" of who we are, to feel the power of the "special and surprising message", in Santayana's words, audible in Catholic living, to recognise "the bias", or "orientation" (as we would say today) it gives to life, and "the vistas it opens up" and "the mysteries it propounds".

Our aim in doing this is to pass over more freely, intelligently and redemptively into "the other world we live in". This "other world" is often dispiritedly seen in contrast to what we call "the real world", almost implying that our faith populated an unreal world. In this context, the other world means this real world revealed as founded in God and open in the hope to a summation that will be the healing, the keeping and the fulfilment of everything we have judged real or found worthy of love.

Such good people who drift in this direction think it is possible to start all over again, to improvise a new general Church in which we are all just Christians together. A general amnesia, whatever its diagnosis, has never been a particularly creative state. We become new by owning and, in some ways, disowning our past; by continuing the hopeful exploration that marked the centuries that brought us forth; by asking forgiveness for the strains of the destructive conflict, timidity and spiritual meanness that have been interwoven into the lives of even the brightest and the best.

Secondly, the identity that concerns me is not that primarily that is given to us by non-Catholics, however necessary all kinds of dialogue today might be. Let me give an example. I find myself rebelling against the growing uncritical use of the term "Roman Catholic". In fact, an American Scripture scholar, recently in Melbourne, in all his talks referred to the "Roman Catholic position". Americans really have no tradition of using the term "Roman Catholic". But it's become the accepted thing now. I regret this, though I've got nothing against respecting the ecumenical etiquette of this in certain circumstances. This description was imposed on us in post-Reformation England; and was, indeed, made a condition of Catholic emancipation. Not only is it not used in most of the Catholic world, but "as an Australian Catholic of the Latin rite", living in the Archdiocese of Melbourne, while also being a member of an international Religious Order, and even though I gladly celebrate communion with the Pope as Bishop of Rome, and accept his Apostolic Ministry, even so, I do not feel that this is the time to live with such a local designation.

Why? First of all because it obscures the current ecclesiastical emphasis on the local and regional Church. I would be happy if the *Roman* Catholics were Roman Catholic. Papal Primacy does not demand a cloning of the Roman Church everywhere. This was the problem of the Ultra-montane and romantic loyalty to Rome that especially characterised France and England of the last century.

Secondly, because this term, "Roman Catholic", obscures the identity of the eighteen rites that are recognised within the Catholic Communion; a wonderful rich diversity of liturgical, canonical and theological tradition. Very importantly, these rites represent the other patriarchal centres, Alexandria with its Coptic and Ethiopian rites, Antioch with its Syrian, Maronite and Molankar rites; then the Byzantine family of rites (nine of them), Ukranian, Bulgarian, Georgian, Greek, Serbian, Italo-Albanian, Melchite, Rumanian and Russian. Then, there are the Chaldean and Malabar rites, not to forget the Armenian rites; and finally the Latin or Roman rite! So there are eighteen rites, and we're just one of the many. Why should all this universality be suppressed by an indiscriminate use of the adjective "Roman"?

Thirdly, when we Catholics have surely been called to be part of a much more global world in all the quest for liberation that entails, I find the word "Roman" far too narrow in describing the mission of the world Church. More about that later.

For the moment I fear the growing uncritical naming of

119

ourselves as "Roman Catholics" is a restriction and theologically unwise. Needless to say, if other communities in the Church Catholic wish to use the adjective "Catholic" (for example, the Old Catholics or the Anglican Catholics) I cannot object, but I would lovingly keep asking, "why"? I don't see why we should be the only ones with an identity crisis!

But if I object to the blurring of Catholic identity through amnesia and if I'm uneasy about having "Roman" uncritically used about us, it will be as well to admit that I can see no future in an abstract definition of what we Catholics are. There are, of course, distinctive Catholic Doctrines, Theological positions and practices. These can be defined. Still in being so defined they do not express the whole Catholic identity as I am envisaging it. For along with the point of dogma is a Theology, indeed many Theologies. And nourishing Theology and challenging it is the ever-teeming tide of Catholic experience expressing itself in symbol and art and sacrament, in devotion, mysticism and doctrine. Such is a whole field of compact meaning fed by different cultures, different ways of life, different vocations, different frontiers of mission and levels of practice, different communities large and small. Catholic identity may be explored, sensed, celebrated, even rejected, but I doubt if you can define it; especially now when in purely demographic terms most Catholics by the year 2000 (two-thirds) will not be in Europe or North America, but in South America, Africa, parts of Asia and Oceania.

Theology was so used to defining its faith in dialogue with European agnostics (the unbeliever); it is now being formed anew as it tries to speak for, and to, the oppressed non-person in these southern parts of the world. In a situation of terrible poverty, political oppression and deep faith, its "public" is non-European (and often non-white) in cultures that abound in religious sense.

Catholic identity is changing because its people are changing. It would be a very abstract Theology that would really think it could define what is happening as other cultures, new political experiences, new prophets and martyrs and thinkers make their presence felt. It is not an abstract identity but an historical one; as the Catholic Church experiences a vast demographic shift in its membership. More obviously for most of us, it is moving out of defensive isolation and into deep dialogue with other Christian churches and other religions and world views. There is no formula capable of expressing such dynamics. Still, though we may not be able to express such an identity adequately, we do not mean that we do not have one; that we do not live it; that we cannot share it.

So far, then I have argued that Catholic identity is not ideally dealt with either by the emptiness of amnesia, by imposition from the outside or by abstract definition. How then are we to approach it? Not by neglecting it, not by passively being called this or that, not by some logical exercise, how then? The answer has to be in terms of our consciousness as Catholics, above all, what is most important in our consciousness, the move towards conversion as we become more fully, lovingly, wisely, and redemptively what we are called to be.

But, how can we begin to think about such an identity? What are we called to be? From what I have been saying, I hope that I have already hinted at the way I am conceiving of this identity. If we take models from modern psychology we find that identity is generally considered as a dynamic affair. There is the one identity, but developing through now subtle, now dramatic interactions with a social environment. But persons, if they're to live out their potential, must negotiate many stages, through birth, childhood, youth, adulthood, middle-age, old-age and death. And not without pain, contradiction, and tensions perhaps lasting decades of our ordinary lives. Evidently there are no instant persons. And what Newman noted: "in a higher world is otherwise, but here below to live is to change, and to be perfect is to have changed often". What Newman recognised in his rhetorical way, psychologists such as Eric Erikson have elaborated in, say, his much cited eight stages of human life cycle.

For the life of any individual develops from that little

bundle of clamorous needs, to the generativity and wisdom of a self-actuating maturity.

Similarly, in terms provided by the critical philosophy of Bernard Lonergan (see *Method in Theology*, DLT, 1972, 6-13 and *passim*), we can track the development of true selfhood. It is an on-going process of self-realisation. It unfolds in the dynamics of self-transcendence. For our humanly authentic self comes into being by first going beyond mere impressions and experience to questions of meaning. It unfolds beyond meaning to questions of truth. And it even goes beyond the world of factual truth to questions about what kind of human reality we really wish to form. We have to come to a point of self-determination. We have to opt for values. Through such an option, we form a moral world. But that is not the end of it. Hidden in the search for any meaning, and implicit in the commitment to any values lie the often repressed questions: What is the meaning of all our search for meaning? What is the ultimate value of all our commitment to values?

To such generally accepted psychological and philosophical models of the self-in-becoming, we can add the biblical notion of identity through vocation. We are who we are by God's call. Like Abraham, like the People of Israel, like the prophets, like Mary, like Jesus, like the disciples, like Paul, we have our identity by being called beyond what was less than the full promise of our lives, into a richer, fuller ultimate life. This not without suffering and taking up the cross. It involves giving one's life for one's friends, one's enemies, "the many", the world itself — if Jesus is any model for us. It is a calling into a pilgrim existence. John says in his first letter, "It has not yet appeared what we shall be; but when he appears we shall be like him, for we shall see him as he is" (1 Jn 3, 2).

Such an identity is an exodus and a passover. For the sake of "the one thing necessary" it leaves behind a lesser version of self, to save the true self by letting the false self go: "He who hates his life for my sake will keep it unto life everlasting".

Understandably, the psychologist and the philosopher would

shy clear of these dramatic biblical expressions. Nonetheless, identity through change, a self-realisation through self-transcendence, a self-becoming through various stages of dying, suffering and even renunciation, is a common theme.

Admittedly, it is a little imaginative to apply these models of individual becoming and the phases implicit in them to the Catholic identity of the Church. But they do afford a clue to something there in the corporate life of the Church, comparable to the phases of individual development.

Just to admit this possibility is of value. It cautions us against allowing into authentic Catholic identity elements that cannot authentically be kept. The first of these inauthentic elements is everything we include under the general term, "sin": bigotry, ignoring human rights, greed and lust for power, lack of faith, despair, hardness of heart. The second inauthentic element is everything covered by the designation, "sickness": soured feelings, suspicion, resentment, overdependence, defensiveness, narrow-mindedness, fear of the feminine and the female, sexual obsession, authoritarianism. . .

Further, this awareness inclines one to admit that various features can be quite authentic at one stage, say, when the Church was under fierce cultural and political attack in the Europe of the eighteenth century, but, at a different stage of history, they can and must be transcended. Such a "different stage" would be the present situation compared to post-reformation, Enlightenment Europe: we all share a terrifyingly threatened world, with the first priority going towards growth in the direction of a more global and just humanity. In this sense, the Church is not only in need of doing penance, but also in need of reform: the "confiteor" always introduces the Eucharist; and the Pilgrim Church is increasingly aware that we have here no lasting city (See *Lumen Gentium,* ch. 7).

So, I would say this: any interpretation of Catholic identity which understands itself as a process of becoming, and of moving out from previously formed provisional images of itself, is far closer to the truth than a dogmatic identity that would declare itself to be fixed, final and fulfilled. The Pilgrim People is in a state of becoming. It is an historical self maintained only by a movement of self-surpassing. We cannot ignore this mutation in the Church's self-understanding. It is an institution. As such it is a vast, social, historically venerable and religious reality. But, more biblically and more personally, it is the reality of a People, a Pilgrim People, finding itself, finding by growing, letting go, adapting, expanding and renouncing, as it enters creatively into each context of its mission.

This shift from institution to People necessarily makes any identity less easy to define. When "it" becomes "we" identity consists more in following a vocation and keeping a good conscience, in the faithful, responsible living out of what we discern ourselves called to be. Such an identity is always more than our capacity to articulate it. For it is made up of our free actions in responding to God, and being open to his infinite Spirit, collaborating with the Saviour of the world, in the challenge of mission. It is an all-personal Church, "a people made one by the unity of the Father, Son and Holy Spirit" (*Lumen Gentium* 1).

It is, if you like, you and I and all of us, who are creative agents within the identity of the Church; you affect the "we believe" of Catholic identity in a unique way. A more personal identity means a far more responsible identity. This responsibility is evident in the openness, adoration, the self-surrender and the self-donation to the all-personal mystery of the origin, centre and end of our belonging together.

Such a responsible identity implies a continuing conversion. It means being drawn beyond ourselves by grace, and going out of ourselves in love and action. It is a multi-level conversion; a conversion to God away from idols and demons; a conversion to the common good away from self-serving interests; a conversion to truth away from narrow-mindedness and error; a conversion to our most creative selves, from the familiar pathologies of our fears, permissiveness and ritualism.

I don't think it would be forcing the issue by suggesting that each of these inter-related levels of conversion can be tagged, as it were, with one of the traditional marks of the true Church, one, holy, catholic, and apostolic. Catholic identity must become more "one" by being converted to the Trinitarian mystery which is the foundation of its communion and mission. It must become more "holy" in its involvement in the common global good. Our Catholic identity becomes more "catholic" with its openness to all truth; and finally, I would suggest, that it becomes more fully "apostolic" by being converted to its true creativity in the particular situation. A shift of emphasis, you would have already detected not so much the four marks proving that the Catholic Church is the one true Church; but now ways of conversion, of becoming more the Church, in its full sacramental power and vocation.

So at this point, before going on to reflect more on the identity in this four-fold conversion, we must face an objection which has perhaps been nagging at the "good Catholic" in all of us. How can you talk about the developmental self-transcending identity of the Catholic Church, when, undeniably, in the terms of Catholic belief, it is the true Church? It's all very well to bring some relativity into Catholic identity. But it remains embarrassingly clear from classic Catholic sources that the identity of the Church is to be Catholic, and the identity of Catholics consist in being the Church; and this Church, acknowledging the Pope under the presidency of duly consecrated and appointed Bishops, is the one true Church. Doesn't this massive Catholic article of faith impede any development in Catholic identity, save that of having more people baptised or making their submission to Rome?

I think any serious Catholic, struggling for an authentic appropriation of the Faith, must feel the force of this starkly stated objection. Are we not stuck with the worst of both extremes: to keep and defend an exclusive identity on the dogmatic level of faith, and to lose it, or worse, be involved in the pretence of giving it up in the context of ecumenical and interfaith dialogue? Like it or lump it, the massive Catholic dogmatic identity cannot really afford to shift, it would seem. The only way forward is to be more of the same. They, out there, no matter how much we love or respect them, must eventually come to the point of assuming our identity, not we, theirs . . .?

Such a sentiment, crudely expressed, but maybe deeply felt, explained a lot of Catholic diffidence and rigidity. What can creative belonging really mean for us? How then can we responsibly liberate the Catholic believer in all of us to hold, in the one identity, both a sense of the unique grace that the Catholic Communion is; and the honest search with other Christians and other religious believers in order to grow into something more? How can we be honest at both points? Is our former assured Catholic identity based on an error? If it were, what we are trying to say now to ourselves and before the world is that we were wrong and now must put it right with a more limited notion of our identity. It makes a difference if an error is of the heart of our identity.

You see, it is not just a problem of a loss of conviction, or a more liberal ecumenical theology. It is a problem occasioned, indeed provoked, by the text of Vatican II, as for example, we would have in *Lumen Gentium,* Chapter 8 and *Decree on Ecumenism.* For the Council says not that the Catholic Church *is* the "true Church of Christ, but that true Church of Christ *subsists* in the Catholic Church governed by the successor of Peter, although many elements of sanctification and truth can be found outside its visible structure". Because all these elements "properly belong to the Church of Christ, they possess an inner dynamism towards Catholic unity".

Clearly, in teaching and in practice, we are being invited to re-interpret Catholic identity in a more open way. Does that mean that the former, rather exclusivist self-understanding of the Church was wrong? This, for example, tended to allow for the salvation of non-Catholics not because they belong to other Christian communities or religious traditions, but in spite of such belonging. But now, what before was absolute, appears to be relative; what before was firm and as fixed as a rock, now looks like an electrical field, as it were, attaining a greater or lesser intensity in a variety of Christian ecclesial forms.

It would be a long story to attempt a thorough account of how and why the shift came about. The barque of Peter, of course, moves on; the winds of history now blow differently; the tides of culture now run in a different direction. The boat is made of so many new products; the crew have had wider experience; the ocean has been more thoroughly charted and in many ways the weather is more ominous. Though we Catholics might pride ourselves on our "winged keel", the old self-assurance of sweeping along with full spinnaker would simply tip us over. We have to try another tack.

In other words, we live with a vocation worked out in history, and our identity is achieved through self-transcendence. "To be perfect" means "to change often", if we are to keep on being a sacrament of grace for all. But not only have we, our Church, our world changed; we can better name and discriminate the facts and qualities of change (P. Chìrico, "Dynamics of change in the Church", *TS* 39 (1978) 55-75.) The language suitable for, say, the Europe of the one Catholic Church in the Middle Ages, the rhetoric understandable when for religious and political reasons that one Catholic thing was sundered and divided, the position developed when Christians practically had no contact with Buddhists or Hindus or Moslems, in a world where the village atheist was just one step up from the village idiot — such languages do not serve us now unless we are more intent on self-serving at the expense of serving the universal mystery of Christ. For the Word became not a Catholic, but man; a man uniting himself to every human being through the incarnation (see *Gaudium et Spes,* No. 22 and John Paul II *Redemptor Rominis* No. 8). In other words, we have more evidence of God's action in other Christian communities and religious traditions, and see their integrity of faith and love. The old black and white distinctions will not do. We must learn to name reality more subtly, more comprehensively, more redemptively. To the undiscerning snow is just snow, leaves are green, and a camel is a camel, and you either hit the ball or miss it. But for the Eskimo, whose world is snow, I am told there are some twelve words for white, because it makes a difference, if it's a firm-white or soft-white, whether you live or die. For the Arab, there's quite a vocabulary for camel: size, shape, age, strength, colour, odour, etc. And I am told that amongst some jungle-dwellers in Africa there are eight or nine words for green, a green world of many shades. Just as for the cricketer you don't just hit or miss: you drive, cover drive, on-drive, off-drive, you glance, you snick, you hook, you cut, you back-cut, square cut; you steer, you block, you tickle, you pull, etc., etc.

A precise situation and intense iterest demand that you distinguish. So it is with the language of the Church. We are part of history. Our vocation keeps on being a vocation. Our God-given identity keeps on realising itself in many stages and contexts. Any identity, as Erikson suggests, passes through eight stages; and even Shakespeare's Jacques has it in *As You Like It,* we have the "seven ages of man". This is the fundamental meaning of Vatican II's new language. It is trying to locate our identity in a more redemptively creative way within the grace and the development of the ecumenical and inter-faith context. Not to attempt this, is to define Catholic identity as a fixated, congealed, defensive thing, floating above history and impervious to the unsettling Spirit of Christ; and unwilling to risk love.

Now, after that brief excursus, we return to the dimensions of conversion inherent in being a Catholic today: one, holy, catholic and apostolic; a conversion to God; a conversion to the common good; to truth; to apostolic creativity.

One:

Catholic identity is marked by unity and oneness. Such an integrity, in all its articulated complexities and diversities, in all its community of mission, in all its self-possession and relatedness to other communities and traditions, even to other Faiths, is grounded really (when all is said and done) in surrender to God, the one all-reconciling mystery. It is on the highest and most intimate level of conversion, a surrender to "the One", the one mystery of God. This consists in reducing all its teaching and practice, all its prayer and mission to radical adoration. Catholic identity can only live from the totality of the mystery of a self-giving God, the mystery of forgiving Grace for all, Father, Son and Spirit.

It might seem at once obvious and strange, but, funda-mentally, I believe we Catholics must adore; and surrender ourselves to what we adore. We must listen to the silence beyond all our words and our most essential definitions. We must taste and inhale the reality of a world-transforming love in all our sacraments. We must yield to a mystery always bigger than ourselves. We must learn to entrust ourselves far more intimately and unreservedly to the Grace that we so confidently administer.

To the Catholic mind this comes hard, to be poor, adoringly poor, in the midst of the extraordinary richness and variety of our tradition; to possess by not possessing in the midst of our enormous organisation and resources. It is time for Holy Mother Church to let her more disreputable Sister, Holy Wisdom, the familiar of mystics and disturbing prophets, take the lead. The lovely book of Rosemary Houghton called *The Catholic Thing,* is a good reference here.

The challenge to focus on the "one thing necessary", the meaning of all our meanings, stands out more clearly when we ask, what are our familiar Catholic idols, the idols that demand too much human sacrifice at the expense of human healing and human encouragement? What are our familiar demons possessing us and locking us in patterns of self-destruction?

Our idols? Surely the very system, perhaps the very richness of tradition and forms of law and words and morality and even certitude that can be a long way from the heart of God and the heart of man. A cult of the Pope will not save us, only love can save us. The Papal Ministry, surely one of the charisms of the Spirit, serves the mystery of the living God but never substitutes it. The law of Sunday Mass, surely a reasonable and hallowed community discipline, can legislate no Grace if there is no joy in the infinite abiding, all-healing mystery we eat and drink in the Eucharist.

Our demons? Our anxiety to be too certain, to place spiritual security above love, to multiply acts and observances and organisations and plans and devotions for fear that, finally, there might be nothing and no-one there. A tendency to take on our poor selves the salvation of the world. There is only one saviour to whose salvation we must witness, whose saving power we must celebrate, but whose universal design of salvation we dare not limit. We live now in a world infinitely more vast and variegated than our predecessors imagined. We need consequently to be open far more to the real dimensions of God.

It is a terrible risk, in a way, to let our idols topple and our demons to be driven out. Instead of a Father-God who is the infinite legitimation of a worldly and ecclesiastical authority, we find the Nameless One who is invoked as "Abba", who refuses to reveal himself in any way other than through the crucified, defenceless humanity of his beloved Son. He gave himself for the life of the world in solidarity with the poorest, the weakest, the lost.

Instead of the Lordly Christ reigning in power and communicating earthly triumph to the Church, we are left with the defeated, rejected Jesus, who refuses to his last cry to be anything but the witness to a universal mercy. Whatever the Resurrection means, it does not mean exchanging the rough ugly wood of the Cross for a bejewelled cross of gold, the ornament of the affluent and the talisman of the secure.

Instead of the forgotten Spirit, occasionally invoked as an optionally extra consolation, we Catholics now have to adore the unsettling wind of power and flame. The Spirit is the infinity of open creative love existing between the Father and the Son. He is not administered by our rites, our laws, our traditions; he is not contained by the bounds of our present catholicity. His wholeness is infinitely more: and it must be he who administers us.

In short, on the level of conversion, the point where our identity is held ultimately together, we have to adore the Trinity of divine persons revealed in the reality of the cross. Only *there* is our hope of Resurrection. To pursue the ways of such a God is not to lose our identity but to find it in the darkness of silence and the overwhelming creative communal history of God himself. If, in these times of ecumenism and meeting other faiths and other hopes, we will be accused of adoring God and trusting his love too much, the worst that will happen is this: we will be found to be in the company of mystics and saints, who like Therese of Lisieux had "hopes that touched upon the infinite".

Perhaps it is high time we became the People of God.

How miserable any reflection on Catholic identity would be if we left out God! And how sanctimonious it would be if we left out the concern for the human, the moral dimension of living with and for others in freedom, justice, peace and love. "How can we love God whom we cannot see, if we do not love our brethren whom we can see?" — to cast the words of St. John into a question.

Holy:

A new level of religious conversion to the real God implies a new dimension of moral conversion. For adoration means union with God redemptively at work in the world. With a converted religious identity comes a new moral identity. We are being inspired to be "holy" in a new way. Catholic identity has, of course, always lived close to its saints, its apostles, confessors, virgins, martyrs, reformers, pastors, doctors and founders. We have canonised them as permanent irradiations of the Spirit in the Communion of Saints.

The saints never cease to be saints, of course; but there is a question that is worth asking at this moral turn in our meditation on Catholic identity. Who are our saints today? And what are they inviting us to, even if they are not formally canonised or perhaps even dead? I would imagine names like John XXIII or Oscar Romero or Dorothy Day or Mother Teresa or Lady Jackson or Helder Camara would be mentioned. Each one of these was or is an outgoing Catholic in some way, looking beyond what was to a greater Catholicity of what might be. It makes us all think about our Catholic moral values.

There is a distinctive Catholic experience of morality, something like the rules of the club. We are stricter than others about sex, divorce, contraception, abortion, family obligations, etc. We seem to think that if we keep the flag flying the world will be a better place, and I'm sure it would be, given the threats to the high values of human integrity in the delicate ecology of the moral world. But there is something more, infinitely more. For the journey *inward* to conquer the devious territory of the seven deadly sins in the name of Christ, has taken up so much of our Catholic spirituality and moral concern. What Pope and Bishop and the Prophets of our age are calling forth in us all is a journey *outward,* out into the terribly threatened world of violence and loneliness, family breakdowns, political oppression, de-humanising poverty, discrimination in all its forms and a jeopardised environment. Practising virtue can no longer be thought of as some private soul culture. Rather, it means being virtuous (virtus, power), being full of the Spirit's power and the love of Christ, to throw in our lot with the whole of threatened humanity.

This new kind of holiness means a new kind of moral wholeness which in turn implies three Catholic qualities. I would suggest that these are compassion, collaboration and hope. Compassion: the need to have a more Catholic heart, truly sensitive to the dimensions of the demonic evil that tortures our poor world. If you add up distinctively Catholic positions, they tend to be prohibitions — understandable in a particular tradition of morality, a regulation of individual lives, a personal code.

Yet behind the particular distinctive issues has been an inspired love, what theologians called the Catholic *caritas,* a universal charity far larger than the refined distinctive moral positions that mark us. The cry for justice and peace, a cry arising out of compassion for the poor and the forgotten, is being heard more and more. It has been growing this past hundred years from *Rerum Novarum* on, through *Gaudium et Spes, Populorum Progressio, Redemptor Hominis,* the prophetic statement of the American Bishops on nuclear disarmament, *The Challenge of Peace. Gaudium et Spes* gave classic expression to the turn in Catholic moral sensitivity and occasioned an outbreak of Catholic social concern. This responsibility is intimated in its opening lines: "The joy and the hope, the grief and the anguish of the men of our time, especially of those who are poor or afflicted in any way, are the joy and the hope, the grief and anguish of the followers of Christ. Nothing that is genuinely human fails to find an echo in their hearts. Christians cherish a deep feeling of solidarity with all human beings and their history" (*Gaudium et Spes* 1).

Our personal asceticism must be re-interpreted as a training in self-forgetfulness in an effort to be open to the needs and sufferings and problems of the world we live in. The image of the Catholic Church as the pillar and ground of truth needs to yield to that of an international community of really Christ-like love.

I ask myself so often if our splendid, exalted morality has often made us so self-controlled as to be self-preoccupied, so as to become self-centred. But our neighbour now is all peoples and regions and oppressed states. It may be centuries before we can show all the earth the face of Christ and speak his word. But now surely is the time to treat all with the love of Christ, to be a sacrament of that love. Our central sacrament, the Eucharist, "the summit and the source of all the life of the Church", is a celebration of our solidarity in Christ. But, note, it is not only the real presence of Christ present under the appearances of bread and wine, it is a real presence made possible by sharing the food and drink of our lives: "The fruit of the earth and the work of human hands". As long as poverty and degradation characterise so much of the world, the Eucharist is a judgment upon us all, inspiring that compassion on all who suffer. Compassion, of course, is pure emotion if it is not collaboration.

Let not our ultimate vision of the new heavens and a new earth make us less energetic for the building up of the actual world we live in (a familiar refrain of *Gaudium et Spes,* Nos. 40, 42, 43). It is for the Father "to determine the time and the seasons", not us. In the meantime there is work to be done: peacemaking, protecting the environment and caring for the forgotten, restraining technocracy to a human proportion, protecting family life. All this pre-supposes an enormous collaborative effort in bringing a human world, a globally human world into existence.

The poor of the world are the Church's neighbour. With the urgency and extent of the task it is not enough to preach values, not enough to cultivate morality as a private set of rules. The religious, cultural, educational and the political presence of the Church must become a moral force for the humanising of the world, a force of holiness for the wholeness of our human being together. When, say, in the Middle Ages, the Church and the world were one, this happened automatically. With the Reformation and the Enlightenment the Church retreated into its own religious enclave. It was often heard as a voice resistant to democracy, human rights and freedom. Now it is different. It is increasingly obvious that the Church is becoming for millions a voice and a force for freedom (for example, the Philippines, East Timor, South Africa, South America, Poland and even the recent development in the United States). That's an extraordinary thing; in fact, it at least proves that not all multi-nationals are evil! The vast proportion of Catholics, enmeshed as we are in the social and economic structures of our countries, live still with a very individualistic morality. And when we are confronted by such leadership towards a new human and global morality, our former roles (as, say, despised minorities in society trying to prove that we are good citizens or obedient children in the Church waiting to be told what to do) make us ill-prepared for this new moral responsibility, the new way of living the holiness of the Church. Nonetheless, from the Pope down to the little "social justice group" that meets in the Parish, the leadership is there: an invitation to pursue a more comprehensive, a more freedom-affirming and world-making morality.

No, it is not to exchange heaven for earth. It is rather to make the earth open to its final fulfilment. A Church indifferent to the suffering world, projecting an image of God concerned for only respectable citizens does not make the prospect of the eternal banquet of heaven very attractive.

That brings me to the third point of Catholic moral identity, hope. We Catholics have always been characterised by a patience with the complexity of the human condition. To devout Protestants we often do not appear to be radical enough. And we don't seem to be religiously intense. Well, that may be true, but still the good side of that is that we do not lose hope for anyone. And even our doctrine of Purgatory is a strongly hopeful statement: we don't need to be saints all at once, not even when we die. I think there's a beautiful Catholic grace, sacramentally enacted in the particular sacraments of reconciliation and anointing that we should explore and celebrate far more.

Still, the weight of moral issues, the dimensions of the oppressions and the discriminations we have unwittingly imposed or suffer, can appal and paralyse the modern conscience. We can all appear to be caught in a terrible web of sin and violence and be crushed with the weight of responsibility. But even now "God is greater than our hearts", and the mystery of healing and forgiveness is greater than all the responsibility or guilt that we feel. The old Catholic distinction of hating sin and welcoming the sinner has never been more necessary. The Church has to be more a home to us, especially today when the life-threatening proportions of the world we have made tend to make it a less friendly place.

There is in fact a whole line of great women mystics, St. Hildegarde, St. Gertrude, the two Mechtildes, the two Catherines, Julianna of Norwich, Marie of the Incarnation, right up to Therese of Lisieux in our century, who refused, from the radiant hopefulness of their lives, to put any limits on the infinite mercy of God. True, an established necessarily masculine theology did not often hear their voice. But it is a deeply Catholic one: "All shall be well and all shall be well, all manner of being shall be welll". This is not the time, in a torn and broken world dreading our powers of self-destruction, to be reasonable about the folly of God's mercy. These great women are perhaps inviting their fellow Catholics to re-centre our limited, calculating morality (so often offering only bad news to the haunted and confused), in the morality of the crucified: the self-giving, incarnate expression of God who is love.

The more we Catholics can become that part of the world, alive to its limitless hope, the more we will mediate the healing power of redemption as Teilhard de Chardin said: "The world belongs to him who offers it the greatest hope".

I look forward to seeing Catholic identity, Catholic morality, Catholic holiness bloom as a great hope for the world and all within it, no matter what the depths of their guilt, their self-hatred, their despair. Let us be holy, as the healing of the whole world.

Catholic:

Then there is the third mark of the Church, Catholicity. The explicit aspect of Catholic identity, it points to a third level of conversion — openness to the whole, the total truth. It means a passing over from narrow-mindedness and unwillingness to listen, from bigotry, prejudice, congealed positions, suspicion of free-enquiry into the opposite of such failures of intellectual integrity. I'm not implying that such negative qualities are characteristic of the Catholic mind, at least of the authentic tradition of Catholic thinking with its Augustines and Thomases and Pascals, and Newmans and Von Hùgels, Karl Rahners and Bernard Lonergans.

Still, there was a problem. The power and conspicuous attainment of one stage of our history was celebrated and clung to for too long. New philosophies, new areas of scholarship, the incredible development of natural sciences, the modern disciplines of sociology, psychology, anthropology and all the rest of it, all burst on us, each to challenge the great Catholic system of thought in a new way.

The example of Thomas Aquinas, receiving all the tradition of the Greek and Latin Fathers to re-express it all in the categories of the pagan philosophy of Aristotle and using to that purpose commentaries from the Islamic and Jewish sources is a long way from the sorry history of Modernism at the turn of this century; and, say, the disciplining of Teilhard de Chardin a few decades ago.

Our intellectual history has vacillated between an extraordinary creative openness and narrow-mindedness (often wearing the mask of pastoral concern).

In short, broad-mindedness, the universal cosmic vision, is a Catholic thing — never finished, always opening up to fresh vistas. Very significantly, using the example of Aquinas adapting the philosophy of the pagan Aristotle, Dom Helder Camera a few years ago, suggested that we need a new Catholic theology, at least in the world within which he

136

lives, to articulate itself in terms of the atheist Karl Marx ("What would St. Thomas Aquinas, The Aristotle Commentator, do if faced with Karl Marx?" *The Journal of Religion* 58 (1978) 174-184). The point is that the intellectual component of Catholic identity can never be convinced that creation is evil. For the Catholic mind everything retains its radical goodness, even if it is ill-used or distorted.

The point to make is that there is a Catholic intellectual confidence, native to our identity. It is always a struggle to keep it there. One modern thinker, David Tracy, has characterised the Catholic mind as an "analogical imagination". (See his *The Analogical Imagination,* Crossroads: New York, 1981). Intrinsic to Catholic identity is the drive to express our beliefs in a rounded objective affirmation of the real. It pre-supposes a confidence in the human mind to make faith reasonable, articulate, all embracing, Catholic. Behind all the pluralism of our experience, all the data and conclusions of modern sciences, is the whole reality, the infinite mystery in which everything can be related and brought together. All of "nature" is related to "grace", all of existence has been owned by the Incarnate Word and penetrated with his presence. The mind does not live in a narrowly religious world. Faith liberates us to explore the incarnate mystery manifesting itself in all creation. Any exploration of meaning is a step in the celebration of the meaning of all meanings. "All things are made in him, through him and for him".

Everything is revelatory of truth, a step to the truth of all truths. The self-transcendence achieved in any act of knowledge lives implicitly from an orientation to all truth. Indeed, to establish any fact, any truth, by appealing to its sufficient reason, is only possible if there is some prior sense of the infinite truth for which we were made, the sufficient reason for all our sufficient reasons, the meaning of all our meanings (see Karl Rahner, in the same issue of *The Journal of Religion*: "Thomas Aquinas on the Incomprehensibility of God", 107-125).

A philosophical point, perhaps: but the mark of the Catholic mind has been realism, a critical realism born of faith, faith in God, who does wish to be our fulfilment —

but not by destroying or overwhelming what we are as intelligent beings; but by "healing, perfecting and elevating" our intelligence.

This kind of Catholic mindedness, this "analogical imagination" attempts to see the whole in terms of inter-connectedness grounded in the one mystery of God's love. This envisages all reality emerging from, and leading to, the infinite truth.

It is deeply relevant today. There is a minor relevance. The minor relevance is that of the Catholic Education System. The tradition of Catholic intellectuality we inherit can never be content with teaching students secular subjects merely as an occasion for forming them in the faith. The reverse is the authentic position, from Justin to Origen, from Augustine to Thomas, from Erasmus to Pascal, from Newman to Von Hugel, from Chesterton to Lonergan. We form students in faith by opening and enticing them to explore reality with all the wonder and all the rigour they are capable of. The God who is the elusive rather boring object of "the religious education period" is not the incarnate cosmic mystery of Catholic faith. Could it be that powerful influence on Catholic identity, Catholic education, is looking for a philosophy? And that a diagnosis of its philosophy might find that in recent centuries or recent decades it has lost its sense of being precisely a philosophy — Philosophia, a love of wisdom? With the consequence that Catholic education, like all modern education, has lost itself in the flat monochrome world of facts, endlessly stored, endlessly retrieved without going through any mind — so to leave so many blithe young spirits starved of wonder and unacquainted with the adventure of intellectual exploration?

The major relevance for the Catholic analogical imagination is the exploration of the universe of truth. Never has human history been so confused and enriched by so many contacts with so many cultures, by the findings of so many sciences, by so many new abilities at its disposal. The understandable tendency for any mind conscious of more and more "unknowing" and the limits of its knowledge, is to collapse into a sense of hopeless relativity. How can we ever know the whole truth? The best we can hope for is to pick up now this fragment, now these facts, now these suggestions and to use it for what it's worth. If, however, the deepest instinct of the mind and heart has already found its home in the infinite mystery and if that instinct has been transformed by faith to identify the human face of that unutterable reality in Christ Jesus, then there is a centre and a focus. For we have the ultimate human sense of the universe: it has a divine coherence; it has a Christened consistency. No matter how many ways are put forward to explore and establish the real, they all focus on that "omega point" revealed even now in "the love that moves the sun and the stars" (Dante). A self-giving mystery of limitless love alone guarantees that the universe does not become a no-man's land, weird and de-humanised and lost. For it shows that it is a home-land where the mind can wander and play as it will. Truth is an infinite space to explore, uncanningly complex: yet at the end of exploration wearing the smile of a human face, "It is I, do not be afraid".

In effect, I am suggesting that Catholic identity has nothing to fear from the vast and variegated world revealed in our day, as long as it is an alliance with all truth-seekers. "The truth hurts", we sometimes say, but it is only the partial, the fragmentary truth that hurts and confuses. The whole truth heals and makes for unity and reveals itself to be our native land.

Apostolicity:

Finally, the fourth mark of the Church: apostolicity. Founded on the Apostles, those originally sent to East and West as the authentic witnesses to Christ. This mark points to the fourth element of conversion — conversion to our actual mission, a repossession of our creativity in the here and now; in all the particularity of time and place and the people that we are.

Here I suggest again three points bearing on our topic. First, an idealised general apostolicity, looking back to what the Apostles did, must not paralyse us in regard to what we must do now where we are, I mean, here in Australia.

I mean that we must be Australian Catholics. In being such, I mean that we must express our faith in the sounds and the silences of this precious land, where Christmas is in summer and Easter is in Autumn (if there are seasons at all). The land with all its deserts and plains, its oceans, its rivers, its eerie vastness, its endless bush is our eighth sacrament. And its people, with their power and hope, and inarticulate search for the fullness of life, their embarrassment about religion, their wonderful capacities for friendship, irony and loyalty — they are our people.

To be a Catholic is not to be in a spiritual space-capsule, circling the earth, belonging to no place, released from the gravity of down here, "down under". We have never had a special confidence about being Australian Catholics. Perhaps we would have done better to read John O'Brien's poems, or Ed Campion's *Rockchoppers* or Vin Buckley's *Cutting Green Hay,* or the poems of our eminent Catholic poets. Jim Tulip, a professor of poetry in Sydney, remarked that many of our major poets are or were Catholics. He suspected it was our sacramental sense. Whatever about that, we are *sent* into this place with these people, to live and celebrate the Gospel with them, some of whom in recent decades came from a hundred other countries to find a more human life with us. And others, the black Australians, preceding their and our arrival by perhaps 50,000 years, stand in our midst as witnesses to the vastness of history and the Providence that guide us all. They challenge us both to care for this great land and to be converted to a fuller justice.

Then, there is the second point about being converted to mission. The former clerical and hierarchal organisation of the Church has broken down — "there are simply not enough priests to go around", we often hear said. Still, other types of ministry and other types of competence in the Church are emerging, an especially remarkable fact in Africa and South America and even here amongst us. The Holy Spirit seems to have answered all those prayers for vocations by spreading his gifts more widely. The theological point that has emerged is this. As the People of God, we are all responsible for the

Church, all part of the mission of the Church before we have the diversified ministries within that mission.

This came home to me when I first read Pope Paul's *Evangelii Nuntiandi*. I think there are about eighty-two paragraphs in it and only two paragraphs refer specifically to the ministry of priests and bishops.

That's an extraordinary theological message. The whole document dealt with the responsibility of the whole people of God to witness to the Gospel, a responsibility that is lived according to different graces and different vocations. The issue for Catholic identity is one of negotiating this shift in apostolicity. Neither theology nor the actual urgent situations allow us to place so great a load of responsibility on our ordained Ministers. They will obviously continue to exercise their pastoral ministries; but that will need to be far more in the context of a community of ministries where no one of us can do everything, but all of us must do something, if we are to be marked by the apostolicity of the Church. I think conversion is not too strong a word if it means growth in Christian maturity which asks not, "why doesn't the Church do something?" (or Father so and so or Bishop so and so), but "what can I do?" I am Church, we are Church.

There is, of course, a grieving thing. The old ways die and the old resources dry up and, in particular, great priests are spread so thin — that's a sadness. But the sorrow can be turned into joy, if only we can find it in our Catholic selves to realise something of what St. Paul was getting at when he says "to each is given a manifestation of the Spirit for the common good" (1 Cor 12,7). Where I teach Theology only a quarter of the 470 people doing courses are studying for the Priesthood, and half of that overall number are women; so people are entering into the Ministry in different ways. Catholic consciousness is, in fact, changing, and that is an occasion to own creatively a broader apostolicity.

That brings me to the third point, the final one, in conversion to mission. There have always been in the Catholic Church, at its heart transmitting its life, magnificent women. Holy Mother Church, and the Church as the Spouse of Christ, are profoundly feminine symbols. They have always been

141

dramatically related not only to Mary, but to the Teresas, and the Catherines and so forth — but more routinely to the millions of women of faith who have been such a high proportion of the Catholic Church. Despite such a deeply feminine mystique and such a predominantly feminine membership, I'm not sure if we have begun to recognise the needs of women, the role of women, the gifts of women, the mission of women in our Catholic identity. All the twelve Apostles were men, but it does not mean that women either then or now need to be systematically excluded from the many public areas of the Church's life. Here we obviously need some kind of healing. We need as a Church to join the human race. Peter has always depended on the all-faithful presence of Mary. He fled and denied Christ and returned to serve and finally to die for him. I wonder if he would have done that if Mary's faith had failed? But it didn't, and she remains in the Church as an invitation to us all to be redeemed to a full humanity of being in Christ "in whom there is neither male nor female" (Gal 3,28).

I must stop here content merely with alluding to one of the deepest challenges in Catholic identity today. What is it then? It is this: becoming what we are — one in God, wholly for humanity, Catholic in concern for the truth, apostolic in a new creativity in the context of the modern experience. I have not spoken about Catholic identity in self-justifying terms. It is no longer a matter of congratulating ourselves on being one, holy, catholic and apostolic. It is becoming a matter of proving that we have been so marked by grace in a new readiness to share it in an all-embracing love.

11

The sacrament of marriage

THERE IS a distinctively Christian way of speaking about marriage for, besides being a social agreement or contract, it is a "covenant". By this we would mean that, in some deep fashion, it reflects the love and tenderness of the Covenant between God and our humanity. And there is a distinctively Catholic way of speaking about marriage: marriage is a "sacrament". By this we would mean that marriage, along with a number of other sacraments, embodies in a special fashion, the presence of Christ in the public life of the Church.

"Sacrament" is about the most intense and comprehensive word in the Catholic theological vocabulary. It denotes a range of meaning that attempts to express the intersection of the divine and the human in Christian existence. By "divine" is here understood the Mystery which has appeared in Christ, a Love redeeming and life-giving. By "human" we mean that which is natively apt to reveal the divine character to us: for the "Word became flesh", claiming as his own, in an intrinsic irrevocable way, what was before, inescapably, promisingly but always ambiguously, "ours". The divine is now apprehended, in the incarnational economy of Christ, to be revealed and communicated in the depths of the human. The ultimate dimension of human experience is grasped as a being-in-Christ, in the Spirit of Love, in the presence of the Father.

To say that marriage is a sacrament is to reverence the sexual love existing between man and woman, in all its dimensions of faithfulness and fruitfulness, as a participation in the ultimate Mystery of Love. It is saying something about the Church's commitment to the divine in the human: God must be sought through what we are. Our hopes for humanity are infinitely extended through what God has revealed himself to be. Marriage stands in our midst as a "visible sign of invisible grace". And grace is the "healing, the perfecting and the elevating" of the whole human character of the marriage relationship.

The word "sacrament" applied to marriage indicates our understanding of the manifold meaning of this reality: a human relationship of love participating in God's Being-in-Love; a human capacity for self-fulfilment alive with the dynamics of the dying and rising of Christ; a human experience of limitation and vulnerability open to a transcendent redemption; the care for spouse and children yet part of the mission of the Church; an obvious physical union and ecstasy yet anticipating a new creation when God will be everything to everyone. A "great mystery", indeed.

For all its being a participation in a great mystery, a visible sign of invisible grace, it remains a "sign", a provisional reality, clothed with the ambiguities of our human situation. Marriage embodies the mystery, but it also presents problems; and the sociologist, the psychologist, the anthropologist can observe and list them.

First, there are the problems we might call *institutional*. In the mobile, complex technological world, marriage necessarily is evaluated as a traditional institution. Modernity commends the values of creativity, adaptability, variety, freedom. Marriage, for all its elusive permanence, does not seem to promise such values. It is not, it would appear, at the cutting edge of our culture.

The pop dramas of our media seldom select marriage now as the "happy ending". More predictably it is the man and the woman with the courage to break away from the restrictions of family and social mores that have the hero's part. What a former age would have called adultery, fornication, perhaps even perversion, is now apprehended as the necessary self-fulfilment in a sincere love. The massive superstructure of modern life is weighted against the exclusiveness, the

144

commitment and the permanence of marriage. Far more likely, such features of the marriage relationship would be dismissed as an inhuman restriction, a banal routine of home duties, the sacrifice of one's creative self. The more sophisticated the society is in technological terms, the greater the statistical probability of divorce. Civil law tries to adapt to the given facts. Whole classes of professionals are employed to deal with the problems of marriage: with a certain neutrality, they seek to repair what is not irretrievably lost in the relationship. And, when there is nothing to be saved, they facilitate the decomposition of what was before a family unit.

The Mystery may remain in the proclamation of the Church, but the problems of the married are foremost in the minds of modern people. The unattached trend-setters are hailed as leaders; and the "sexually-liberated", confessing their incapacity for life-long relationships and choosing sterility, are understood to be the creative people.

The institutional breakdown intensifies the *existential* experience of the problematical nature of marriage. For so many of our contemporaries, marriage has been a destructive experience. A breakdown of marriage is necessarily an experience of disillusionment: the promise of perhaps rapturous early love could simply not be kept. The triviality, ugliness and dreadful incapacity of human relationships showed themselves in ways that were not suspected. When one experiences such intimate bitterness and betrayal, the great human words promising love, acceptance, forgiveness, faithfulness must come to mean almost nothing. And the children born in such marriages have received their terrifying early lesson: the love that brought them into existence is not be trusted. They have necessarily been taught, that despite the sincerity of good intentions, human relationships are a very precarious affair.

If we are to continue to speak of marriage as a sacrament, it must not be at the price of making light of the hurts that have been suffered in marriage. Thousands of our contemporaries, out of their experience of guilt, fragility and even betrayal, will have their own instinctive speech in speaking about the meaning of marriage. For us it may be a manifestation of an infinite Love; for them it was an intimate, devastating experience of the problem of evil.

There are the institutional problems, the existential experiences, and there are also theological aspects of the problematical character of marriage today. Very obviously, marriage no longer draws its meaningfulness from a religious world view. No longer does it have a necessary place in the public life of the Church, neither to be inspired by its preaching nor affected by its sanctions. It is up to the married couple, first of all, to make of marriage what they can. The marriage counsellor replaces the priest as the significant helper. The counsellor, the lawmaker, the therapist, the educationalist are permitted, in our culture, to appeal only to the empirical level of "human relations" in assisting the couple's expectations of what marriage should be. Religious meanings are not available in the social life of a secular culture.

Paul Ricoeur, as one amongst many, points out that the secularisation of marriage has been a long and gradual process.[1] Paradoxically, the desacralising process began when the religion of the One God triumphed over the erotic nature-religion of the Baalim. Greek Philosophy followed on and contributed to the extinction of the ancient polytheism. Western culture, prizing spirit and suspicious of body, acknowledged the social significance of marriage in the divine plan. But it seems to have been caught between two sets of symbols: that of the demon of sex that would turn every man into a rapist and every woman into a harlot; and that of Genesis that would acclaim God making man in his own image, "male and female he created them", the radical goodness of sexual existence revelatory of God's relationship to mankind in the Covenant, indeed even as this is climaxed in Christ's relationship to the Church as his body (Eph 5,32).

Today, the tension remains. A demonic erotomania leaves a voyeuristic culture unable to work out what is wrong with hard-core pornography even for children. Yet a religious vision of sexual dimension of life has not only to prove its case in a situation in which no evidence is admitted of a transcendent reality; but also it must cope with a culture still affected by the "great masters of suspicion". A religious view of marriage must be able to cope with, say, a Marxist suggestion that it is nothing but a typical bourgeois effort to gain respectability in the eyes of the oppressive establishment. Similarly, the religious view must withstand a Nietzschean rage asserting that Christianity is the great life-denying force perverting all our exuberant vitality into a timid banality. Thus, too, the Freudian suspicion remains that a religious view of marriage is nothing but a fundamental fear of our sexuality, a neurotic union of the psychologically underdeveloped.

It appears that the reality of marriage is projecting many images. The "good image" is, in principle, everything we have said about marriage as a sacrament. The "bad image" flows from the institutional, the existential, the religious breakdown in a world cut off from its ultimate resources.

In the conflict of such images the shape of the challenge confronting us becomes more clear. It is not merely to assert cool-headedly that marriage exists now as a secular reality in a non-religious world, even though we must admit that a long perduring religious epoch has definitely ended. This has left our era in a kind of cultural dark night of the soul, unable to find direction in the images and concepts of tradition, yet more and more experiencing that the one-dimensional world of our techological making is not the whole truth. We have tasted the truth that makes us slaves, the truth of the technological, totalitarian ideology. We seek again the "truth that will make you free".

The issue is the resacralisation of marriage. How can we reinsert it as a free, creative, meaningful relationship into the life of a purified faith and a fresh experience of God? In the meantime, marriage, Christian marriage, goes on, the often unacknowledged experience of thousands of couples still finding union, fulfilment and a hope to hand on to their children. This is the time for theology to stay especially close to the experience of married couples, perhaps to see its role less in the formulation of a doctrine about marriage, and more to facilitate the ability of married people to speak about themselves, to give witness to what they are, to what they have found to be true and healing and life-giving. Theology must learn to be an expression of their creativity.

This brings me to two types of remarks. The first will deal with the character of contemporary marriage experience, the second will indicate some points for the reformulation of a more adequate theology.

One technique for heightening our awareness of the real bearing of faith's experience is that of suggesting "limit-experiences". Unless the right context is established; the Gospel sounds suspiciously like the parroting of old answers. Once, however, we advert to the unsettling edge of our experience, faith's meanings begin to be creative: quite literally, they begin to make sense. For these "limit-experiences" are the points in our lives where the normal, routine experience breaks down. In times of grief, joy and astonishment, we are so often left with nothing to say; we are taken to the outer edge of our existence, "drawn out of ourselves" in the direction of . . . what? A surrender to a more complete truth, or a sinking more deeply into absurdity: these are the only options.

When theology suggests such "limits" in our lives, it aims to clear the ground for a renewed appreciation of the revealed answers we have received. These cannot be a creative element in our lives unless we are in touch with the questions we are living. The aim is not to prove the reality of faith, but to liberate its capacity to speak to us in what we are going through. The Word makes sense when we are living beyond ourselves, at the limits of our very limited humanity.

There is a great range of limit-experiences present in marriage. At such moments the couples (or individuals) can commit themselves to a great depth of meaning in their relationship . . . or sink more deeply into absurdity. Theology must develop its ability to articulate the originality of what married couples are at present experiencing, especially when there is so much in modern culture that "routine-ises" our humanity into that of the "Mass-man", where the celluloid image is taken as the norm of life; the true experience of the limits of our experience, the "agony and the ecstasy" are suppressed.

The following series of questions might, quickly and evocatively, help to earth the sacramental meaning of marriage in typical "limit-experiences". In the interests of greatest sense of reality, we would address them directly to a married couple:

Marriage as Participation in God's Being-in-Love: What did it really mean for you to "fall in love"? How is it that your spouse was revealed as so attractive? What is it that has so drawn you together? . . . For a lifetime? Does the attraction and surrender of love take you deeper into reality . . . or are you really living an illusion? Does your love give the most real glimpse of the beauty of the other . . . or is it all blind, biological instinct? Does your love give you a privileged view of the world and one another, or a false one?

Marriage as the Anticipation of Eternal Life in Resurrection: Can the love that brought you together be, in any sense, forever? Does it last beyond growing old, suffering, incapacity, death? Does your love anticipate the fullness of life together, or is it a hopeless projection, a prelude to nothingness and separation?

The Grace of Marriage: Dare you ask such an absolute love from your spouse? Are either of you worth it? What worth is there in me that I can ask and give a lifetime love? What has made me worthy of such a love . . . capable of it? Where is it leading to?

Marriage as Healing and Redemption: Am I losing myself by being so tied down? Am I surrendering what is most personally my own? How can I cope with the layers of selfishness and hesitation that are revealed in me . . . my terrifying inability to love, my fear of being lost and eaten up? How do I remain hopeful? How do we keep growing together?

The Fruitfulness of Marriage: What do your children mean to you? How are they yours? How are they a gift? How are they not an increasing threat to your independence and capacity to enjoy? Why do you accept such responsibility for others? What kind of world are you bringing into existence? What sense of life are you handing on? What kind of life are you preparing them for . . . to be survivors in a lonely, hopeless world? More than that? How much more?

Such questions locate marriage in its range of limit experiences. In the light of such heightened awareness, theology

149

must press on to articulate Christian meanings as comprehensively as possible. This takes us to the second remark, and the final one.

What we are really looking for is a new sacralisation of marriage in the "Spirit-ual" reality of the Church. Marriage has been struggling against an inadequate conception of God as "Supreme Father" sanctioning it from above, recognising it as part of his plan, helping it with the grace won for us by Christ. We can see now more clearly that such a view of the divine is not only utterly unbiblical, but also owes more to the Deism of the Enlightenment than to Christian theology.[2] A revitalised theology of marriage might express itself in the following pattern of development:

The Spirit is the life of the Church: only in the Spirit can we recognise Jesus as Lord. Only in the Spirit are we taken into his relationship to the Father, "whom no man has ever seen" (Jn 1,18).

In the Spirit we encounter Jesus as Lord in the depths of the human: there we meet him as the Incarnate Word. In the power of the Spirit we discern the bread and wine of the Eucharist as the Body and Blood of Christ. In the same Spirit, the Christian couple meet one another "in Christ", healing, perfecting, elevating their union. In the same Spiritual awareness, the whole Church celebrates this marriage as "sacrament", the reality and sign of the healing, redeeming presence of Christ among us.

Thus, Christian marriage is not, in the first place, a structure imposed on the couple from above, or from the outside. It is rather a union inspired "from within" by the Spirit who enriches the Church in a variety of ways: the couple find one another in Christ; the Church finds in their union a manifestation of the Spirit and an embodiment of grace.

In this more "Spirit-ual" understanding of marriage, it is easier to grasp the ecclesial bearing of married life. Each Christian marriage is a charismatic gift to the Church in its mission to the world. This helps to clarify our speech about marriage as a vocation, for it is a vocation to participate in the mission of the Church in a special way. Just as the

Priestly Ministry is better understood by complementing its "Office-ial" character with a charismatic, Spirit-ual dynamism, so also marriage. By inserting it into the charismatic structure of the Church, its role in the Church's mission of evangelisation is enhanced.

Conclusion: These reflections will no doubt be a further indication why marriage is always the test of Christian theology, for we are forced to extend our capacities to talk about such a breadth and depth of the human whilst at the same time speaking of the special character of the Incarnate Word. It might confirm the reader in a conviction that theology is always the despair of marriage, for it is either too romantic or too uninspired. Let us keep doing our best: for after all, all marriage is about the way a couple says "we" and mean it. Here we have suggested that in a world of such promise and much alienation, that this couple can say "we" the way God says "we", in the unity of the Holy Spirit. Consequently the depths of their union and the breadth of their conversation are never quite exhausted.

1. In *Sexuality and Identity* (ed. H. Ruitenbeeck) Dell: New York, 1970, pgs. 13-24.
2. *Cf.* especially the work of H. Muehlen, as, for instance, in *Entsakralisierung,* Shoeningh: Paderborn (1970), above all pgs. 473-505.

12

The great conversation between Jesus Christ and Karl Marx

THE VATICAN'S *Instruction on Certain Aspects of Liberation Theology* (August 6, 1984) was quite a "media event". And not without a predictable amount of confusion.

It has been commonly spoken of as condemnation of liberation theology which, of course, it is not. You can certainly hear the voice of the conservative side of the discussion in South America, notably that of Bishop Alfonso Lopez Trujillo. He has long insisted that Marxist analysis always tends to draw you into the whole system with its atheism, anti-religiousness and doctrinaire class struggle.

Still, it does help to read the document in question. Those, especially busy journalists, who may not have had time to get through the 35 pages of the text, could have picked up the following points from the first two pages:

(i) Liberation theology, as a reflection on the "essential truth of the Gospel as a force for freedom", is described as "full of promise".

(ii) This instruction is concerned with those who use certain Marxist concepts "without sufficient critical caution".

(iii) A positive statement on "the vast theme of Christian freedom and liberation" is promised.

(iv) This warning should "in no way be interpreted as a disavowal of all those who want to respond generously and with an authentic evangelical spirit to the "preferential option for the poor".

It would be well to keep such points in mind. If an international Church wants to distance itself from an ultimately dehumanising version of Marxism, it is not necessarily a sign that its social concerns are lessening.

Everything depends on how this statement will be used. It can be exploited as a generalised negative judgment on the social involvement of the Church in South and Central America as though this is evidence of being duped by international Marxism. Or, it can occasion further dialogue and clarification.

Over the centuries there have been problems with Christian faith elaborating itself in terms of secular systems of thought. Thomas Aquinas' condemnation by the Archbishop of Paris for being too Aristotelian, 700 years ago is always a wholesome reminder.

More recently, Church authorities have had concerns relating to the theological use of Freud, Existentialism, Historical Criticism and so forth.

Then, from the other side, since most liberation theologians have been very insistent on breaking away from a dependency on European theology for the sake of an indigenous style of reflection, it can be no skin off their noses to be challenged to distance themselves from the more sorry experiences of European Marxism.

Nonetheless, the controversial point is Marxism. Indeed, just what is Marxism now? In *Pacem in Terris* (*Peace on Earth*), Pope John XXIII made the distinction, 20 years ago, between "false philosophical teachings on the nature, origin and destiny of the universe and man and the ever-developing historical *movements* which have economic, political and social ends which have arisen from such teachings.

"The *teachings* remain the same, but the *movements,* insofar as they conform to the dictates of right reason, and are the interpreters of the lawful aspirations of the human person contain elements that are positive and deserving approval".

True, not a very subtle distinction, but a useful one in this context. Surprisingly, it was not used in this document. Marxism is more than the errors or shortcomings of the original Marxist theory.

Then, too, if your experience of Marxism is marked by

the Soviet occupation and subsequent oppression of Poland, you are hardly likely to be enthusiastic at the prospect of such a "liberation" taking place in South America. And if, despite such an oppressive experience, you are able to write, as in the case of the present Pope, what to many appears as a Marxist document, *Laborem Exercens* (*On the Meaning of Work Today*), with all its emphasis on the priority of labour over capital, workers' participation in the ownership and means of production and the profits that result, and the role of trade unions as "the mouthpiece of social justice", you may rightly suspect that the discussion is not over yet.

To take the broad view, what we are witnessing today, in this convulsed era of the world, is a conversation taking place in the presence of two of the great classic figures of our civilisation. Whether you follow them or not, no one remains uninfluenced by them. They are Jesus of Nazareth and Karl Marx.

The first is more remote historically, but, for millions, in the evidence of their faith, he is a living presence. He still speaks: "Truly, I say to you, as often as you did it to one of these, the least of my brethren, you did it to me" (Mt 25, 31-46).

The "least" with whom he is so identified, are the hungry, the thirsty, the naked, the stranger, the prisoner. The God whom he involved and invoked in his tragic career was the God of the forsaken and the powerless.

He showed the face of a God who was really intent on human freedom, willing the healing of all human ills, calling forth hope.

His witnessing to such a God resulted in his public execution. At very least, he was a prophet of hope and a martyr for the forgotten and the outcast.

To follow such a man in the explicit commitment of faith, or merely to feel the power of his fascinating presence in a post-Christian world, is to meet a challenge. No one can face him without being forced to ask, who is my real God? No one can pretend to follow him without being involved in some responsibility with the "least of his brethren".

If, in the experience of faith, you come to recognise him

as the revelation of God with us, then it is a very subversive God that one adores: One who is met only at the price of solidarity with those our ordinary world so easily excludes.

If, for others, he is simply there as a fascinating historical figure in the memory of our fragmented civilisation, he still stands for the possibility of a hope, a compassion, a form of humanity about which our modern world has all but despaired.

To feel the presence of such a figure is to be confronted with one's own selfishness. It means, too, that we have to work harder on our self-justifications. . . .

The other classic figure is Marx. He died only one hundred years ago. He was no saint nor even a particularly lovable man. But he stands for something, an unsettling presence, one of the great "masters of suspicion" when it comes to looking at one's place in the complex powerplay of our times.

He embodied and endlessly expressed one powerful, original insight: so much of human suffering is caused by the economic structures that, by favouring the privileged few, degrade and exploit the many.

He occasioned a re-reading of history in the light of the self-justifying ideologies of vested interests. He grasped the possibilities of human freedom as a concentrated social force able to shape human destiny, not without conflict and revolution, into some final form of justice.

He diagnosed the mass poverty of his time as an instance of capitalist greed living from the creative and unrewarded energies of the toiling masses of humanity.

Such a pattern of exploitation fabricated its own self-justification, pressing a compliant religion into its service. As long as God offered a reward in another life, the mass of mankind would accept its dispossession in this life.

His solution was to change the system. His method was to inspire the freedom of the dispossessed as a world-shaping force. With such new energies unleashed, society would be turned upside down, and justice would result.

Marx had no room for Jesus. He was the possession of capitalist religion. The issue, in the conversation of which liberation theology is a part, is whether or not Jesus, living

155

in the reality of those who follow him, has room for Marx. Can the analyses and methods of Marx be redeemed to a more human proportion, given the dreadful history of the crimes committed both in the name of Marx and of Jesus?

One thing is clear from any reading of the Gospels. Jesus was more intent on the human rights of the poor than on the "divine rights" of kings, emperors, religious leaders or the powerful of the world.

How this conversation will end, I am not sure anyone really knows. What is clear is that, either as participants or listeners or eavesdroppers, we are all increasingly involved in one of the great conversations of our time. A crucified Jesus and a revolutionary Marx still speak to the millions who, even in their sufferings, sense the presence of a new freedom and the stirring of new hope.

It seems to me that what we call liberation theology conducts its conversation along the following seven lines. They may provide a useful frame of reference.

1. Self-Determination

In a real and obvious sense, the human world is rapidly becoming a world-that-is-brought-about through our free action. The social force of emancipation movements, in all their variety, work for a more free society.

Environmental issues arise now since nature itself enters into the scope of human decision. Most dramatically, this new capacity for free self-determination occurs in regard to the issues of peace and war: we can choose the probability of self-destruction by allowing the proliferation of nuclear weapons.

All in all, the human world is a self-determining reality, no longer a regular order or a blind fate that simply occurs or is imposed.

Liberation theology is a modern style of thinking inasmuch as it has grasped that the social and economic order are the result of choice, and that human freedom is truly human only when it is liberated to participate in the formation of the conditions that govern human life.

2. The Political Nature of Freedom

No one is "above politics". Not to be "political" is a political decision to ratify the status quo. The only choice one has, is either to be politically critical or naive about the reality of social life.

This counts especially for the Church: to refuse a political stance on human rights is simply to ratify the politics of those who degrade or oppress human beings. Hence liberation theology attempts to liberate the Church for constructive political involvement.

3. Praxis

We know the truth by doing it. In many ways, this active understanding of truth goes back to Aristotle: abstract definitions about the human good always arise out of conduct and experience; they mean nothing to the uninvolved.

In a sense, because so many branches of learning have realised that truly human knowledge is more than simple information, liberation theology is just one instance of "liberation thinking".

Education is increasingly aware of its duty to contribute to the self-actualisation of the person rather than to stuff heads with information, just as modern medicine is trying to remind itself not to look merely at a body with certain symptoms of disease, but at the whole person and the whole process of healing.

The major instance of the demand for "praxis" is science: the quality of the human reality, the presence of human values, must govern the "objectivity" of science; otherwise, as the presence of the nuclear threat continually reminds us, science dehumanises, and becomes a brute alienating power.

And so with Christian truth. It is meant to be lived, acted, to have a life-transforming effect. It is rightly suspect if it has no social consequences, or even has evil effects. In such instances is the believer really knowing God and the power of grace?

Lest it degenerates into a nice construction put onto an

unredeemed reality, Christian truth, in the judgment of liberation theology, must be tested in action; what power has it to promote human freedom and give hope to suffering human beings?

4. The Dangerous Memory of Jesus

Classical theology was often content to deal with the uniqueness of Christ by using abstract notions such as divine and human nature, hypostatic union and so forth. Liberation theologians point out that the reality of these classical affirmations should make us aware of the truly human life of Jesus.

He was not an "abstract human nature" but a free being who made real choices. Faced with all the possibilities his time and society offered him, he proved himself a partisan of the poor and the outcast. God was incarnate in *such* a human life.

By allowing the historical content of such a life to influence one's faith now means that Christian belief has much more of a social and political "bite" to it.

5. History from the Underside

The dangerous memory of Jesus unsettles the naive social security of faith. It provokes a more compassionate reading of the history of one's society and one's world.

Uncritically viewed, it appears as the success story of the few. The failures, the dispossessed, the defeated are left on the underside. It is not necessarily a Marxist conviction to state that the surest knowledge of the real state of one's society is revealed by listening to those who are most powerless and most forgotten.

In this sense, liberation theology says that it is the poor who teach theology about what the world is really like and where God is to be found.

6. Social Analysis

The way the voiceless and powerless feel about reality

calls forth a hard-headed look at the society. Here the issue of the use of Marxist categories of analysis has become controversial. If big business or rich landowners control the natural resources, the industrial power and the media of a country, it is hardly surprising that Marxist terms most easily identify the structure of the problem — how the resources became so concentrated in the hands of the few, how ideology functions to maintain this position, how it can be challenged.

If such a use of Marxism makes people sound like atheists at this point, it might be because they are rejecting the false god of the powerful and the rich. . . .

7. Context

All the above points are brought together in a particular context. They are earthed and tested in a particular community experience which is at once the cell of the new form of Christian life and the base for outreach into a wider society.

Liberation theology was never meant to be a truth in the head, but the truth lived with and for others. How far its theological insights can be appreciated "out of context" is a fair question in the current discussion.

When all is said and done, the central value of liberation theology will, I am sure, enter into all theological reflection. For it is this: thinking about God without an involved commitment to your neighbour is an illusion. The real God makes for community and freedom.

This is no exotic conviction. It is all an effort to tease out the meaning of "the truth that will make you free" (Jn 8, 32).

13

Salvation and sacrament: The dimensions of saving grace

ONE OF the benefits of all the recent discussion on Liberation Theology is that we have been forced to explore all essential Christian themes in a new way. The classical formulations of Grace, Salvation, Redemption, Justification, Sacraments and so on are now influenced by a new context.

Theology can no longer be an ecclesiastical version of *Trivial Pursuit*. It has to find a form of expression which resonates with the real problems and hopes of the world we live (and die) in.

For, in some obvious sense, that world seems to be more familiar with the disgrace of human malice and indifference than with grace of a loving God. It knows more about being lost than being saved; more about being sold out than "bought back"; more about self-justifying ideologies than the justification that comes from surrender to God's saving will; just as it is more aware of the signs of religious decline than of sacraments as "visible signs of invisible grace", signs and anticipations of the Kingdom.

So questions keep occurring. How does grace keep on being grace for us, even in the present "disgrace"? How is salvation really an experience of being radically "safe", saved, rescued, made whole, healed, transformed despite the grim inhuman determinisms that affect so many lives?

How real is God's love in confrontation with the demonic powers which seem so sleeplessly creative in devising new forms of greed, selfishness and domination? How does the Gospel keep on being Good News?

Those are the big questions. And they demand large, generous, critical and hopeful answers. I will here make a few remarks on the theme of salvation. I hope that they will serve to sketch the dimensions of the task lying before those concerned to reformulate Christian meanings in a way that will best mobilise Christian energies.

The very word "salvation" has a doubly dubious inheritance. It has become so abstract in its ecclesiastical usage, a long way removed from its original range of reference which is best described in the family of words such as health, healing, wholeness, even salvaging.

It sounds even more abstract when it is usually linked to the salvation of *souls*. The implication is that God's saving love is concerned primarily with the spiritual, the ultimate, a state of vision and communion beyond death.

Though that is an aspect of Christian hope, an exclusively spiritual salvation runs the risk of being no salvation at all. How can it communicate anything attractive or hopeful or healing to ordinary human beings if it is reserved for souls only?

For that reason you will find most modern theologians stressing what salvation is *not,* before they go on to elaborate in a more adequate manner the many-sided meaning of Christian salvation.

For example, they will say salvation is not purely spiritual: it concerns the whole person, in every dimension of our bodily and historical and spiritual existence. It will be pointed out that Scripture speaks more of the "resurrection of the body" than of the saving of "souls", just as Christ's resurrection did not mean that his humanity was somehow vaporised or destroyed, but affirmed, glorified and established in its fullest proportions. He becomes the New Adam, *The Man,* including all human beings in his destiny.

Nor is salvation purely individual. It is a community affair. At no stage in this life or beyond it can we be ourselves outside of relationships with others. For that reason, the Christian understanding of saving grace as it is experienced in the present or hoped for in the future has a strong corporate or social dimension. It conceives of the Holy Spirit as forming us into the Body of Christ, to become the People of God, united in the festivity of a great and final banquet.

Neither is this state of "being-saved" purely passive: something we receive, and that is that. It is an invitation into the life and being of God, Father, Son and Spirit, which is a life of self-giving love and compassion.

In this context, being saved means being set free to be for others. The holiness that results from the healing and wholeness that salvation offers is an activity, a collaboration with the saving love of God for others.

Finally, salvation is not purely "in the end", purely ultimate. It is concerned with the here and now, with the penultimate. It makes a real difference to our experience of isolation, despair, worthlessness, guilt, dread in the present. However fragmentary this seems to be, it is nonetheless a real anticipation of the final salvation Christians hope for.

Such understandings of the salvation are brought home to believers in the Eucharist as the central Christian sacrament. Quite obviously, it is not a purely "spiritual" experience, but a communion with Christ through the medium of our sharing the bread and wine, "the fruit of the earth and the work of human hands". It is not an individual prayer, but a Holy Communion which offers and provokes deep forms of community.

Though we use the phrase "receiving communion" with its implication of passivity, what is really at stake is a receptivity to a Christ and a Spirit which impels Christians to a deeper commitment to their neighbour and their world. And while the Eucharist certainly expresses an ultimate hope for the full realisation of the Kingdom, it is already the happening of an ultimate form of human belonging to God and one another in the ever ambiguous present.

So the Eucharist is celebrated in the Christian community as expressive of the "now — not yet" quality of the salvation that is offered. Though it can be trivialised like all human things, to seem nothing but a mindless piece of ceremonial or a spiritless celebration, it demands to be regarded as the real presence of Christ among us.

It is the essential symbol of how God is acting: the world

is being transformed; the new human community is being formed; the grace of God keeps on being a gift inspiring new energies throughout the course of human history.

It is one thing to criticise defective presentations of the mystery of salvation as they have occurred in the history of the Church thinking. It is another matter to say something satisfactorily positive.

As implied in the above paragraph, the Eucharist compactly symbolises the dimensions of the reality one would like to express. The vastness of the theme leaves any expresion looking very thin. For salvation is about a healing and fulfilment offered to the whole of human existence, individual and social, bodily and spiritual, earthly and historical, present and future.

Still, I believe, the following points are worth bearing in mind when we are drawn into any conversation on what it is finally all about.

First, there is the specifically Christian component. It is not often that one finds this strikingly and comprehensively expressed. The key words here are Father, Son, Cross, Resurrection, Spirit, Church, Kingdom:

Father: The symbol of God as an originating personal love as the ground and foundation of our world and its history. The "problem of evil" is made more piercing for Christian consciousness since it is so penetrated with the notion of God as an all-initiating Love.

Son: God's love is a self-giving movement. It is a self-involvement in the human world. The classical word is incarnation: what is most intimate to the divine identity, "his only Son", the Word, is communicated to the reality of human history. "The Word became flesh and dwelt amongst us" (Jn 1, 14). Because "God so loved the world as to give his only Son" (Jn 3, 16), Jesus can say "he who has seen me has seen the Father" (Jn 14, 9).

The Cross: The divine self-involvement in the world manifests itself as a radical compassion. In the experience of the cross, God knows what it feels like to be a victim. Through Christ, God takes to himself our problem of evil. He is made vulnerable to it as One who knows the seeming powerlessness of love and goodness when confronted with the dark powers that determine human life.

The Resurrection: The love that is revealed in Jesus' solidarity with the poor and the outcast keeps on being love. It is neither defeated by evil nor changed into some form of divine vengeance. This mysterious victory of love as the final form of human life is called "resurrection" in Christian tradition. The beginning of a new order of creation. There is no salvation in a defeated God. The true hope for salvation relies in a Compassionate Love which is inexhaustibly creative, even in the most impenetrable depths of suffering, defeat and death. "I was dead, but behold, now I live for evermore" (Rev 1,18).

The Spirit: This is the Christian symbol of the divine compassionate love communicated to us as a life-force. It is the energy and atmosphere of a new order of life. The Holy Spirit (literally Holy "breath") inspires the same kind of freedom in those who follow Jesus as he expressed in his dedication to the least and the lost of his society.

The Church: The community of those who, through history, follow the way of Jesus and seek to live in his Spirit. It is that part of the world which is expressly aware of the universal love at work in all lives and all creation. To that degree, the Gospel is not a secret to be kept but a saving truth for the whole world.

The Kingdom: This is the symbol which was so dear to Jesus himself. It looks at once to a future state of salvation when God's universal love will be manifest, and discerns signs of how this salvation is already occurring in fragmentary provisional ways. It is the excess that can never be imagined or expressed let alone captured in church-forms. It is what "no eye has seen nor ear heard", the horizon that opens out to the reality of God becoming "everything to everyone" (1 Cor 15,28).

No Christian understanding of salvation would leave out these points, for they are specific to Christian faith. However, the specific points do not make up the whole reality, and I would add just two further remarks.

164

The first concerns our contemporary experiences of salvation — "saving experiences" if you like. The present era is deeply marked by a consciousness of emancipation: — segments of society, classes, races, nations are struggling to break free from structures of dependency or oppression that marked their past. It is an experience of being freed from an oppressive past to be free for a self-determining future.

This social experience of self-determination along with incredible progress of science in combating a whole range of human miseries make it important to find the right emphasis in speaking of salvation in the religious and Christian sense. It is not exactly as though *divine* salvation has been replaced with human "self-salvation", as though God has been edged out in favour of a "do-it-yourself" salvation kit. Our era is far too ambiguous and threatened to give too much credence to the old fashioned humanisms.

Still, salvation, if it is about anything, is about the fulfilment and healing of human existence as we know it. It is the confirmation and expansion of human creativity and responsibility. Hence modern theologies, among them Liberation Theology, continually stress that a divinely-willed salvation, God's gift, far from being incompatible with human creativity and self-determination, heals, confirms and fulfils such efforts.

As the old adage has it, "grace perfects nature". But now *nature* means our whole human capacity to transform our world and form ourselves. For this reason, "the glory of God is man fully alive" (St. Irenaeus) is the most oft-cited statement from the Fathers of the Church in contemporary Christian writing.

A final remark bears on the oddly indefinable character of God's saving grace. The Christian rhetoric of hope is marked by a strange paradox. On the one hand it is full of assurance and authority. On the other, it recoils from saying too much, as though the effort to say too much would be somehow a restriction on what God wants to be for us, as though expressing too much would make God's gifts less attractive. "Eye has not seen nor ear heard nor the human heart conceived what God has prepared for those who love him" (1 Cor 2,9).

Paul's words chime with these from the first letter of John, ". . . we are God's children now, but it does not yet appear what we shall be. Yet we know that when he appears we shall be like him. . ." (1 Jn 3,2).

This reserve about defining too precisely the meaning of salvation has two effects. It keeps Christian hope open to the limitlessness of God's gifts, first of all. But it also contests all the ideologies, be they political, psychological, economic, cultural or religious, which would pretend to deliver us from evil and offer the fullness of life.

For such manipulations of reality not only offer something that is something infinitely less than they promise, they refuse to hear the full tale of human suffering. They block out the usually inarticulate struggle for life and justice of the poor, the agony of spiritual search for meaning, the very experience of the deadliness of death.

No human product or technique is the answer to all this.

So Christian hope typically expands itself to a fullness that can come only from God, to what lies beyond the vision of the eye, the range of the ear or the dreaming of the heart. Yet it remains a hope for a real fullness of life, a blessing on our humanity. So, when it finds any evidence of the flourishing of the human spirit, of joy in being, of the overcoming of evil, it is ready to give thanks.

Salvation is at hand.

14

A plea for the 'poor devils' of the world

I WANT to suggest here the tone of three theological voices speaking from three different continents. Each of them speaks for a deeper inclusion of "the poor of earth" in the Christian Church as most valued contributors to the history-forming conversation of our time. And each voice provokes deep questions for us on this fourth continent.

The first voice, speaking in a gentle contemplative tone, is from North America. John S. Dunne, a noted theologian, teaches in the University of Notre Dame. His recent book is called *The Church of the Poor Devil. A Riverboat Voyage and a Spiritual Journey.* (SCM, 1982). In it, he describes, in a deeply literate way, a kind of conversion he underwent as a result of a journey up the Amazon.

The trip itself, the company he shared on the riverboat, the little shrine he found in Manaus, the festival he took part in at that remote spot, all fused for him into a striking symbol of Christianity as the religion of the poor.

The little shrine that so fascinated him was popularly known as the Church of the Poor Devil. Officially, it was the chapel of Sant Antonio.

Apparently, the "Pobre Diablo" was an illiterate mulatta, Cordelina Tosa. She had built the shrine on the death of the Portuguese cabaret owner, the man she had lived with and finally married. During his life, he had called himself "The Poor Devil". Cordelina adopted his nickname.

When Dunne heard that there was now a black woman named Zulmira who presided some form of African rites at this strange little shrine, he predictably had some apprehensions of devil worship. But on the night he met her, such apprehensions vanished, to be replaced with a vivid experience of warmth, friendliness and a sense of a larger humanity.

He tells what this meant for him — to be taken out of himself, his personal religion — into a new sense of solidarity with the suffering, hope and courage of the poor. He does not speak in terms of dramatic conversion, but leaves us with insights into the Mystery of God as the One who unites us with the heart and soul of the poor, together with a fresh appreciation of the meaning of Christ and Christianity.

He comes to see his faith as "the true religion of the poor" (pg 155).

For him, it is first of all a contemplative experience to encounter the experience of the truly poor — though, he hopes, such a contemplation can be "the heart and soul of action" (ix). He goes on to say:

". . . passing over to others and coming back to oneself, changes one's relationships with oneself and others. And when it occurs among a group of people like those on the riverboat or those in the festival of the Church of the Poor Devil, it is an image of change in human society. It was a way alternative to ways of force and violence. It is the image of a society based on passing over and coming back, on sharing the human essence. . . ." (ix).

Dunne invites the reader to appreciate the necessity of "passing over", in compassion and openness, into the deepest lives of the poor.

Without this passing over, there will never be a common journey, and we will be deprived of the true richness of humanity which "poor devils" possess to challenge the subtler, more deadly poverty hidden beneath our securities.

While Dunne was "passing over" into the soul of the poor he met on his river journey, another voice was speaking, that of Gustavo Gutierrez, a Peruvian priest, one of the pioneers of Liberation Theology.

He is speaking out of the history of South America's oppression and the experience of revolutionary discontent. (*The Power of the Poor in History*, SCM, 1983). The institutionalised violence of that history, and the European "success story" that brought it about, left the native populations mute and marginalised, mere raw material for colonial advancement.

I cannot reproduce here his sophisticated analysis of this complex state of affairs. The main points, nonetheless, are clear: Europe has had a long history, slowly culminating in the exaltation of bourgeois freedom.

Its roots are traceable to such vast movements as

the **Reformation**: the individual conscience asserting itself against ecclesiastical tradition;

the **Enlightenment**: the individual mind questioning all extrinsic authority;

the **French Revolution**: individual freedom asserting itself against an obsolete feudalism and the Divine Right of Kings, to issue forth in such Declarations of Human Rights as: "Every man is free to use his physical strength, his industry and his capital as shall seem to himself good and useful. He may produce what he pleases and produce it as he sees fit".

Of course, this new liberalism aimed at the greatest good for the greatest number. However, it took centuries for the sorry truth to appear, that few, in the global scene, were in a position to avail themselves of this new human freedom. The history of this emancipation meant a terrible oppression for native peoples and colonial lands.

As this spirit of European freedom early manifested itself in *Conquista* of South America, there were voices that spoke for a larger view of human freedom. The great sixteenth century Dominican, Bartolome de Las Casas, spoke out from his experience: "Jesus Christ, our God, scourged, afflicted and crucified, not once, but a million times" (pg 197).

In the accents of such voices, Gutierrez and others like him insist at this later date, that Christians re-read their history. For it has been the history of the "success story" of the few. The millions who lived and died in the "underside of such a history" have been left without a voice.

Hence, one of the major concerns of Liberation Theology is to retell the history of peoples from the underside, where

169

the privileged voice would now be that of the poor, despised ethnic groups, the marginalised and the defeated.

Liberation Theology sees the issue not primarily as one of using the tools of Marxist analysis. The issue is Christian faith. Where is God to be found? The poor, with their often despised "popular religion" invite us to "an experience of encounter with the Lord in the midst of the battles of the condemned of the earth" (pg 208).

This encounter has its own mystical dimension! . . . a moment of silence, a moment of careful listening, to the Lord and to the people. It is a time of contemplation and an experience of joy . . ." (pg 208).

And so by defining themselves into the hopes and struggles of the poor, these two voices, that of Dunne and Gutierrez, despite their difference in background accent and idiom, come to striking agreement. The true God is found in the subversive recollection of the real Jesus who lived to announce "good news" to the poor. . . .

Thirdly, in another accent, from another continent, we hear the voice of Johann Baptist Metz of the University of Munster. (In *Faith in History and Society* (Burns & Oates: London 1980) and *The Emergent Church* (Crossroad: New York 1981). He is a leading exponent of what has become known as Political Theology. He is speaking for the "forgotten people of the Church" who no longer find a voice in the Christian community, now that faith has become so private and the public secular world so flat and dispirited.

He is in a position to witness the massive, silent falling away that has characterised the great churches of Europe. As a theologian, he can live with the scorn of the "intellectuals" and the rejection of society's power-mongers in their estimate of Church.

What is unbearable is the silent schism between the Church and the ordinary people. These, voiceless and powerless, have come to feel that the Church neither speaks for them or listens to them, nor does it enable them to find their voice.

Metz thinks that the Church is paying the price for having protected its people too much. It has offered them a dogmatic orthodoxy but been unwilling to pay the price of a more

170

popular orthodoxy, one in which the usually unnamed sufferings of ordinary people are brought to expression in the name of Jesus, the representative of a freeing and compassionate God.

This is not a respectable orthodoxy, since the real Jesus was regarded as a fool and a rebel by those unconcerned with the struggles of the poor and unimportant.

Metz understands the Church as a movement within history. It is made up of people who neither repress the "dangerous memory of Jesus" nor allow their subversive longings and hopes to be manipulated or extinguished. Such a people are united in a community of hope and in a solidarity of suffering, beyond any ideological or national barriers.

Metz is obviously suspicious of some forms of "popular religion" which do more to induce resignation than inspire freedom and hope (pg 139f). Yet he is deeply committed to the Church becoming a true Church of the people in which one of the main theological tasks would be listening to the usually inarticulate voice of the poor.

It is these "people" (he knows it is a vague word) who must become the subject of the Church — not merely the object of its care. But for this to happen, the whole price has to be paid.

He quotes Peguy: "We must pay the economic, the social, the industrial expenses, — the temporal expenses. No one can avoid that. . . ." (pg 144).

For the Church to refuse to pay this full price of identifying itself with the whole human hope of those who suffer, would mean that Christians merely close themselves up in a kind of "modernism of the heart". This amounts to a private faith trying to keep a good conscience through ineffectual good feelings in regard to the oppressed and forgotten.

And the Church, thus cut off from the genuine aspirations of struggling people, would, at best, merely survive as a "solemn and glorious apparatus" of acceptable religion.

Theology would cease being the effort to bring forth a freeing and liberating vision. It would be nothing more than the ideology of middle-class religion.

Metz's vision is of a world Church including the suffering

people of all nations. Metz envisages the Church as a world community of people ready to contest repression.

No national, let alone any local group, is self-sufficient for whole peoples and nations can easily be denied identity in the brutal power politics of our day. The danger is "a silent disappearance of the subject and the death of the individual in the anonymous compulsions and structures of a world made up of unfeeling rationality" (pg 152). Under such technological control, the human soul, in both its memories and hopes, is threatened with extinction.

To meet such a threat, it is imperative that there emerge a truly world-Church. In it different peoples can bear one another's burdens and share one another's hopes beyond any of the frontiers that history has imposed.

Here, in Australia, today, we are in a position to hear what such different voices are saying. I have barely indicated the rich complexity of the thought implied in each of these instances. Further, I do not think I could do more than begin to suggest how such voices might be heard.

But this much is clear: each one of us must find a place, in any personal religion we might profess, to pass over to the experience of the less privileged around us; and, at least in imagination, make a personal pilgrimage to "The Church of the Poor Devil".

In that moment of quiet communication, we might begin to wonder how our history might be retold "from the under-side", from the point of view, say, of the Aboriginals, or the Asian refugees who are treated to such an ambiguous welcome; or of the unemployed youth or the "useless" aged; or of the forgotten women of our society.

Then we have to ask, what kind of Church, what kind of Christian community we really want to be to counter the inhuman forces still brutalising the history we share?

One thing is certain. The age of successful saints living in splendid isolation is over. It is time for all of us "poor devils" to unite.

15

Purgatory

WE CAN speak of the after life only in terms of symbols. The symbols that are formed in our present human experience enable us to explore, in some dim approximate way, the crisis or fulfilment which belongs properly to the as yet unexperienced future. Purgatory is, then, first of all a symbol. It occurs within the language and imagination of the praying, loving, believing Christian community as it tries to express its hope when confronted with death, guilt and our solidarity in the human condition.

The human condition to which we refer is an horizon which contains the two "black holes" of death and guilt. These are two focal points of the problem of evil, in ourselves and all others for whom we might care.

Christian faith represses neither the deadliness of death nor the terrifying incapacities linked to our guilt. What it does do, in the light of the one single ultimate reality it knows, is to transform this problem of evil into an occasion for entering more deeply, in love and hope, into the mystery of God's Love. For the one ultimate reality revealed to Christian faith is that the crucified one is risen. In Christ, this love has kept on being love despite the power of death and the destructive capacities of our freedom to reject what God has offered. "Nothing in all creation can separate us from the love of God in Christ Jesus" (Rom 8,39).

As a symbol, in such a context, Purgatory is a way of affirming that the transforming power of the Spirit of Christ can still touch us in the darkness of death and in the isolation of our guilt. Like all symbols, it suggests a lot of possible ways of thinking. As a particular symbol of the purification that occurs "after" this stage of existence, it is not unlike other clusters of symbols such as those that occur in the Buddhist or Hindu accounts of the human condition, e.g., reincarnation. That would be an interesting exploration in itself. Here, I will stick to the narrower course, of trying to interpret Purgatory within the explicit terms of Christian tradition.

In such terms it is a symbolic expression of an aspect of the realism of Christian hope. It resonates with our experience of ambiguity: for not many of us, it seems, are fully-finished, integrated selves when we come to die. Love can keep on being love, grace can keep on being grace, even if death overtakes us as unfinished or ill-prepared. It is a way of extending the horizon of human development beyond the stages of "life-cycle" that developmental psychologists such as Erikson discern in gradual growth to human maturity. It is a symbol of both tolerance and hope for the human beings that we are, not as an excuse, but as a way of accepting the patient humanity of God's love for us in our pilgrim condition.

Purgatory is a symbol for faith. It holds God's love, death, guilt and the stages of our pilgrim existence together. And something more, too: our human solidarity with all the suffering, even with the dying and the dead.

The ancient Christian custom of praying for the dead means that we commune with them in their suffering; and stand with them in praying for the full revelation of Christ: Come, Lord! It is an intensification of our Christian hope for the Parousia.

Purgatory is, then, a symbol illuminating the horizon of our faith and hope. But symbols can go bad. They can suffer a displacement of reference which ends in an imaginary literalism which floats away from the original sturdy and discrete affirmation of faith. The rather compassionate, hopeful symbol of Purgatory has been plundered and wrenched from its context to make it appear as lurid factual information about what happens after death. An example of such diseased theological imagination is to be found in a French work of a hundred years ago. It indicates how far the sobriety of faith and the open expectancy of hope can be banished by a silly apocalyptic calculation:

> Suppose you are guilty each day of an average of ten faults. At the end of a year you will be guilty of 3650 faults — to simplify the reckoning let us say 3000. At the end of ten years, you will have 30,000; after twenty years, 60,000 . . . Suppose you can expiate half of these faults by repentance and good works. . . . Now, suppose that each of these faults costs you an hour in Purgatory. Judging by the revelations of some saints, it is very moderate to say one hour. This makes 30,000 hours in Purgatory in all. . . (F. X. Schouppe, **Le Dogme de Purgatoire**, Paris, 1888, p. 93 — quoted by Y. Congar in **The Wide World My Parish**, DLT, 1961, pp. 62f.).

This diseased imagination with its odd apocalyptic calculations is a long way from, say, St. Catherine of Genoa's classical *Treatise on Purgatory* (1510). This great woman mystic does not refer to the torments of Purgatory nor to the duration of their infliction. In fact, she says:

> After the happiness of the blessed in heaven, I do not believe there could be a happiness comparable with that of the souls in Purgatory.

The formal Church teaching on this matter is quite restrained and modest, always being connected with the tradition of praying for the departed. The Council of Trent affirms the existence of Purgatory and underscores our solidarity with the fate of the dead through prayer and the celebration of the Eucharist. It spends most of its time warning against excessive theorising about what is necessarily beyond our experience.

> The difficult and subtle questions which do not make for edification and for the most part are not conducive to piety must be excluded from popular sermons . . . likewise anything belonging to the realm of superstition or smacking of dishonourable gain . . . (DS 1820).

Vatican II introduces reference to Purgatory in terms of the pilgrim nature of the Church, a communion spreading over time and reaching beyond the barrier of death:

> Some of his disciples are pilgrims on earth while others have died and are being purified; and still others are glorified . . . we all in various ways . . . share in the same love of God and neighbour, and we all sing the same hymn to the glory of God (LG 49).

Today's scientific exegesis does not permit any dogmatic proof of the existence or nature of Purgatory. There is, of course, abundant scriptural references to the holiness, justice

175

and love of God purifying the individual and the community. But it would be a false perspective to condense the whole mystery of God's purifying action into the particular Catholic theme of Purgatory as it emerged within the tradition. The various classical references are there: 2 Maccabees 12,39-46 (the exhortation to pray for the dead who have fallen in battle and found to be wearing pagan amulets); I Cor 15,29 (the mysterious practice of being baptised for the dead); I Cor 3,10-15 (the "fire that tests the sort of work each one has done": this has proved to be the most used text of all); Lk 12,59 (the necessity of making full reparation). The context of these and other texts certainly indicate the horizon in which the particular symbol of Purgatory came to be expressed — though, as I say, we are a long way from dogmatic proof texts.

Granted that the fate of the individual soul became a dominant theme only in the Middle Ages, there is a lot in the previous tradition that needs a careful retrieval if we are to arrive at a good modern theology of Purgatory. The two matters I mention in passing are:

1. Whilst both Latin (e.g. Augustine) and Greek (e.g. the Cappadocians) theologies speak of Purgatory in a recognisably traditional sense, the great Origen spoke in terms of a universal salvation and restoration of all things: his theme of *apokastasis.* The whole cosmos and its history would go through a purgation. This was condemned by the Council of Constantinople as a statement of fact. It has never been condemned, of course, as an expression of hope (which was probably what Origen meant it to be). I suspect it is here, within the horizon of hope, that we would find the opportunity for a much vaster theology of Purgatory, more suitable to our understanding of history and the cosmic process.

2. The other element of tradition is the custom of praying for the dead. A beautiful example of this is to be found in the Acts of the martyrdom of St. Perpetua. As she awaits her execution in Carthage, in early March, 203, she is inspired to pray for her young brother Dinocrates, who had probably

176

died without being baptised. Her vision ends "when I awoke and understood that he had been translated from his pains".

It is true that the Protestant Reformers came to deny the doctrine of Purgatory. The reasons for this are, first, because it was so linked to the prevailing abuses in the matter of indulgences, so clearly compromising their convictions on the sheer grace of salvation, "sola gratia". The other reason is more sophisticated. As Tillich complains:

In Catholic doctrine, mere suffering does the purging . . . it is a theological mistake to derive transformation from pain alone instead of from grace which gives blessedness within pain (**Systematic Theology, III, 417**).

I think any Catholic theology today would accept both objections. But as John Macquarrie says:

The kind of suffering envisaged in Purgatory is not an external penalty that has to be paid, but it is our suffering with Christ, our being crucified with him as we are conformed to him, the painful surrender of the ego-centred self that the God-centred self of love may take its place (**Principles of Christian Theology, p. 329**).

If Purgatory takes away from the all-sufficiency of the grace of Christ, it is hardly a Christian doctrine. If it is interpreted as meaning that God's love is somehow conditioned on our merits or suffering, the Christian psyche is soon reeling in hopeless contradictions. The God of such a Purgatory is a very conditional lover, waiting for us beyond death to show us not love but anger: if suffering established our worth in his eyes, an eternity with such a God is a dull, if not dread, prospect.

If, one the other hand, Purgatory is an aspect of the economy of grace and a deeper entry into the reality of God's love, the matter is different. Such love is never changed into something less than itself. Far from pretending that evil is good, or that we have arrived at our best selves, it works for our total transformation. It is a freedom enabling us to be free, a grace possessing us at every level of our stratified existence, inspiring conversion and the full centering of our being on the one thing necessary. Such a love works to penetrate and possess us in every structure and relationship of our human existence. Purgatory is our unfinished existence being possessed by the living flame of the Spirit, to exorcise the demons that have driven us and to cause the idols that have structured our lives to crumble. There is a suffering intrinsic to this: "death upon death has to be endured so that new life may arise". (R. Guardini, *The Last Things*, p. 46).

The following points might serve to suggest a fuller, more Christian approach to the theme of Purgatory:

1. *The Primacy of God's Love and Grace*:

The Spirit of Love, creating, redeeming, reconciling, liberating, keeps on being love at every stage of our existence. Such a Spirit opens us from within to the fulness of life, to bring us to full term in the process of being born as the sons and daughters of God. Under the influence of such a Spirit, we are coming to be, from non-existence to the complete life in God, from selfishness to all the relationships of freedom in God's universe. The Holy Spirit is the "giver of life" in all the states of our existence, everything we call "this life", "Death", "the afterlife" . . . Such Love does not rest content with anything less than our whole free selves in a transformed universe.

2. *The Experience of Love: The Basic Analogy*:

Why the experience of Spirit of Love should be experienced as suffering is illumined by attending to our more ordinary experiences of love. In so many of life's experiences, we receive love as an uncanny gift. It both enlightens and transforms our being. But to the degree any great love possesses us, it makes us aware of ourselves, at some level of our conciousness, as failed lovers, unfree or unfinished, when it comes to responding to what has been given us. Love brings its own suffering, not as something inflicted by the beloved other, but as a pain arising out of the love itself. If love inspires and evokes our best selves, it also brings into our awareness resistance to it: possessiveness, self-absorption, violence, manipulation, limitation. . . . In such a sense, we become aware of our unworthiness in the face of such a gift. "Show me a lover and he will understand" (Augustine) is applicable here. He will understand the pain of not being fully accessible to the other, of not having enough freedom to be completely for the beloved other; of how, in so many deep ways, we fear love and cling defensively and destructively to ourselves. Love brings its own kind of sufferings as something intrinsic to any gifted relationship. It requires its own kind of death and letting go of lesser securities. Purgatory is our encounter with the absolute Love of God as the origin and end of everything we are. In that encounter we experience how we have resisted or disowned what we knew, at the point of faith, to be the living breath of our whole being. And that causes its own suffering and further dying. . . .

3. *Death as Self-Realisation*:

If God's Love is the fundamental principle in exploring the meaning of Purgatory, if our experience of suffering love is the fundamental analogy, the fundamental human fact considered in any theory on Purgatory is death, or better, the significance of the process of dying. The logic of Christian faith inclines us to see death not as a blank dissolution but as an experience of self-realisation. In the moment of death, the human person attains that full individuality which was "in the making" throughout the course of life. All the decisions, options, commitments, judgments of a lifetime finally catch up to the truth that was latent in them. In the action and passion of life we are present to ourselves only in a more or less fragmented, provisional, distracted and usually ambiguous way. The tumbling torrent of life keeps sweeping us along. In death, that restless mountain stream becomes a luminous deep pool. We catch up with the truth about ourselves which, in life, was always ahead or behind us, never completely or consciously possessed.

Christian tradition has tried to make this point by speaking of our being judged in the moment of death. What we are suggesting here, is that in death there is not so much a judgment passed on us by God, but the awareness of full truth of our being: we enter into what we truly are, what we have decided to be, what we stand for, what, through the process of life, we have become. Death is the moment of truth. In it we come to judgment through the evidence that we possess about ourselves. The restless stream of life is finally poured into dimensions which now can fully contain it and reveal it for what it is.

4. *Self-Realisation in Christ*:

In the luminous self-awareness of death we encounter Christ as the key and focus of our human identity. We "come to" ourselves as being made through him, for him, in him. He is experienced as our fundamental identity, the incarnation of all the hopes toward which we had been living.

5. *The Experience of the Crucified*:

If such a self-consciousness places us in the presence of Christ as the absolute determinant of our human individuality, it also reveals the anti-Christ or the counter-Christ which has conditioned our selfhood. In so encountering the crucified, we understand our selfishness and lovelessness in its full light: death reveals to us how we are still refusing to die into the totality of Christ's self-offering to the Father for the life of the world. And Purgatory is precisely the Spirit enabling us to enter more fully into that death, to be totally out of ourselves, for God, for the salvation of the world: it is our final conformation to the crucified, a letting go of all that we are in obedience to the Mystery of the Father, with no other security than that of the Spirit breathing where he will. . . .

6. *Purgatory as Compassion for the World*:

Purgatory is not only a deeper dying into the mystery of God through our union with the dying of Christ. It is worth exploring how it is our liberation for a more complete compassion regarding the suffering world, to the sufferings of which we had contributed in life. Our sinfulness is not only affecting our relationship to the Father, but holding us back from a fully creative immersion in human history: the suffering of Purgatory may well be the process of our becoming truly compassionate beings. It is not an escape from history but a deeper immersion in its drama, crisis, struggle. As I have already mentioned, this may be the point that Christians have most to learn from the myths of reincarnation. Similarly, though one is reluctant to put too much credence in reports of "souls being sent back to earth to undo the harm they have done" and so forth, there may be a deep theological point hidden in such naive expressions: through the creativity of compassion and intercession, Purgatory is our growth to selflessly loving relationship to the world which, in some way, has suffered from the distortion of our own particular history.

7. *The Duration of Purgatory*:

These pointers suggest that it is possible to use two types of language about Purgatory and its "duration": we cannot escape from thinking of it in terms of the temporal duration of our present existence. Granting that limitation of such language, the available rhetorics are reduced to two: insofar as Purgatory is an encounter with the crucified and risen Eschatological Lord, inasmuch as it is a definitive union with the death of Jesus, the language of a "moment" of purification and perfect contrition seems appropriate. From such a point of view, temporal duration makes little sense. On the other hand, if we conceive of Purgatory as a new creative and compassionate relationship with the history of the world adversely affected by our failures in love, then we can speak of it lasting as long as that history. That, of course, confronts us with many paradoxes: is it possible to be "in heaven" (fully conformed to the mystery of Christ) and "in Purgatory" (creatively involved in the suffering of the world, and suffering that suffering) at the same time? Granted that the consummation of the ages has not yet occurred, has theology been inclined to draw too clear a dividing line between the eternal life of Heaven and the state of purgatorial involvement in history? In some sense, we cannot be completely "in Heaven" as long as our sin-affected history continues. And yet, to be definitively and irrevocably with Christ, no matter what the ongoing struggle of history, is a heavenly point of fulfilment.

Though I conclude this reflection with such stabs in the dark, I think the pointers I suggest are sensible enough. A theology of Purgatory will suggest a saving and consoling truth in the midst of our experience of death and guilt if we think of Purgatory as the action of God's love; if we think of purifying suffering as those intrinsic to loving; if we think of the process involved as one of self-realisation in Christ and conformity to his death; if we think of its activity as perfect contrition in ourselves and compassion for the world.

"Eternal rest grant unto them, O Lord, and let perpetual light shine upon them". Creative compassion inspire in them, Spirit of Love, and make them belong to us as fully healed and healing as we follow after. . . .

A NOTE ON LIMBO
THE FATE OF UNBAPTISED INFANTS

Pastorally speaking, the question never goes away: "What has happened to my still-born baby?" — to take one example. A feminine, maternal theology has always implicitly contested the received theological opinion that those dying without baptism cannot be saved. True, Augustine's extreme position of the unbaptised infant suffering a kind of benign hell was modified over the centuries to allow for a natural happiness, yet without the vision of God . . . and, presumably, without final union with those Christians who mourned their child.

What can we say today? The short answer must be: very little. How can we master with any certainty what is so clearly beyond our experience? The only way forward must be in terms of hope. No theology is empowered to state categorically the manner in which salvation may be offered to unbaptised infants. But neither is it permitted to place any limits on the mercy of God "who has so loved the world as to give his only Son". To be left with such a hope, and only such a hope, is not a sign of an impotent or confused theology. A healthy theology knows when to keep silent and to let the mystery come to us on its own terms.

If there were space for the longer answer, we would want to ponder on the significance and interconnectedness of a number of elements in Christian tradition. For example, the Church was never quite as strict on the necessity of baptism as is commonly imagined. Baptism of blood (martyrdom) and baptism of desire (an implicit desire for salvation) have long been regarded as the equivalent of actual baptism in its ritual sacramental form. Has this any relevance to our question? I think so, because these exceptions amount to the Church's conviction that God is not bound by the authoritative practice of the Church. The Church exists to serve, as responsibly as it can, the mystery of grace, not to restrict it. Christ is greater than sacramental forms.

Exceptions to the requirement of sacramental baptism depend, of course, on far more fundamental questions: how real is God's desire that all men be saved and come to the knowledge of the truth (1 Tim 2,16). What is the meaning of Christ's dying to save all human beings (Cf. e.g., 1 Jn 2,2; 2 Cor 5,15)? It is true that we are all born into a state of original sin, that general bias in our history and culture against God and self-sacrificing love. But is it not also true that every human being comes into existence in a universe radically influenced by God's saving action? The grace of Christ is more "original" than "original sin". Which factor most influences the fate of the unbaptised infant: the mystery of iniquity to which it has never consented, or the mystery of grace which it has never resisted?

Within the scope of our freedom, we must, of course, obey the Gospel command to baptise and follow the Church's strict practice in this regard. When, in fact, we can do nothing or have done nothing about the baptism of infants, is our inability or failure so absolutely determinative of the fate of such human beings as to deprive them of salvation? The question seems to reduce itself to our convictions on the character of God and the trustworthiness of the divine will to save.

Contemporary theology seems to sense that there is more theological integrity in humbly entrusting ourselves and all we love (in this case, the unbaptised infants) to the incalculable mercy of a God who is not only "greater than our hearts", but greater than our sacramental rites. (See the judicious but rather timid articles on "Limbo" in *Sacramentum Mundi* and *The New Catholic Encyclopedia*). Any theology, however traditional, that puts limits on the measure of grace is hard put to defend itself against the charge that it has forgotten the mystery it was intended to serve.

16

A hope for Heaven

WITH SO MANY urgent worldly concerns dominating Christian conscience today, it is hardly surprising that theologians have been notably creative regarding the meaning of Heaven.

To speak of "another world" awaiting us when we are so stretched in our concern for this one, almost always sounds like a distraction. Still, despite the apparently limitless space of the potential and challenge of the world confronting Christian creativity, we do come to "limits". Then thinking about Heaven becomes a real and urgent issue. Such limits are death, the terrible excess of suffering, failure, injustice, the threat to world peace and human survival, and, perhaps, most of all, the uncanny ambiguity which shrouds even our best efforts.

In the experience of such limits, a hope for Heaven can be expressed as a radical concern for this world we try to serve. Heaven need not be a denial of the importance of our commitments to this world. Rather, it is the daring expression of our hope for a deeper, more complete way of belonging to the world and its history; it is the language of an ultimate love for life; it implies an ultimate involvement with the Divine and human agents who, in their different orders, have brought this world into being.

1. The Heaven of the Martyr:

One of the limits of human experience which all but demands a hope for another order of existence, is the fate of martyrs. A few years ago, the noted Neo-Marxist Sociologist

Max Horkheimer expressed his hope in an interview entitled, "A Yearning for the Wholly Other". He had this to say:

> Theology means that the awareness that the world is an appearance, that it is not the absolute truth, that it is not the absolute reality . . . it is the hope that the injustice by which the world is characterised will not persist, that injustice cannot be the last word . . . (it is) the expression of a longing that the murderer will not triumph over the innocent victim.[1]

One's very commitment to human history inspires a hope, however tentative, that there will be a moment of salvation in which not only truly human values will be revealed in their authenticity, but also that those who lived by them will be rescued from ultimate failure.

In the light of Horkheimer's remark, it is worth quoting the now oft-cited words of Archbishop Oscar Romero as he uttered them a few weeks before his murder:

> My life has been threatened many times. I must confess, that, as a Christian, I don't believe in death without the resurrection. If they kill me, I will rise again in the Salvadoran people. I'm not boasting or saying this out of pride, but rather as humbly as I can.[2]

Romero saw the basic thrust of his earthly life as an immersion in the struggle of his people. The hopeful logic of his life made him envisage Heaven as the expansion and fulfilment of that involvement. To that degree his sentiments chime with the promise of a far more traditional saint, Thérèse of Lisieux, "I will spend my heaven doing good on earth".

Such expressions are not vulnerable to the old Marxist jibe about Heaven being "The pie in the sky when you die". What they spring from is the most traditional of all Christian convictions, the communion of saints: the solidarity "in God" existing between the "fully living" (the saints) and the "partly living" (those on earth) — whether they struggle in this "vale of tears" or, more optimistically, as members of "The Church in the Modern World".

In short, the reality of Heaven is an urgent issue to those radically and so vulnerably committed to this world and its people. It was certainly so for Oscar Romero; it was made so for those who mourned the forty who were massacred at his funeral. And there is plenty of evidence that it is becoming so for many of our contemporaries who, like Horkheimer, have come to see the world as a splendid tragic question rather than a self-explanatory answer.[3]

2. Irrepressible Questions:

Deep in every human psyche, however great its powers of repression, questions like these resonate, posed as they are by the very terms of the lives we lead: Are we made for life or extinction? Do the values I live for and the causes we find together have a future — or is all this moral commitment a futile gesture in a meaningless void? Is everything we treasure and celebrate together as true life, with all its ecstasies of love and wonder, all its evidence of beauty and daily heroism, all its range of relationship, a promise of a fuller life — or is death the end? Is all the energy of our lives lost in death — or is the dying, so inescapably a part of all care and responsibility, leading into life?

Such questions may be muted or disallowed in a consumer society, but they explode as defiant hope in large parts of the globe where the human spirit is crushed under oppression. And as the prospect of mega-death through thermo-nuclear destruction is vividly portrayed in film after film, millions of people must be wrestling inarticulately with the question: What kind of future dare we hope for given the dreadful precariousness of the life we know?

The way we face, and struggle to answer, such questions deeply affects the way we live now. If living is a journey into life, through all the experiences of dying, into a life finally transformed and confirmed in its love, freedom and relationships, then we are freed to live now. If it is not, then to risk this fragile earthly life for the sake of others, to give our lives to anything beyond the scope of our present securities, is a risk too great to take.

If we believe that true life is leading to a fulfilment in God, then hope for Heaven is both an affirmation of the value of life as we now enjoy it, and a protest against the brutalising forces that degrade or destroy it. In both cases, Heaven is a real issue; and for the millions who are utterly deprived and imprisoned in poverty, sickness, violence and oppression, it is *the issue*. There are times when Heaven is all a Christian has to offer in terms of hope. And there are times when it is the only thing that counts.

3. The "Un-knowing" of Heaven:

It is one thing to assert that hope impels the heart to look beyond any earthly fulfilment. It is something else to say what it is that we envisage Heaven to be.

Indeed, it is striking how agnostic Christian hope is on so many points. Utopias have always offered definite descriptions of human fulfilment. In contrast, the Christian seems almost to recoil from putting into words the kind of fulfilment to which we are called. "Eye has not seen nor ear heard nor the heart of man conceived what God has prepared for those who love him" (1 Cor 2,9). What Heaven might be is, as a rule, communicated in terms of a *theologia negativa*. For "it has not yet appeared what we shall be" (1 Jn 3,2). Further, it is not given to us to know the "times and the seasons" for the final coming of the Kingdom (Ac 1, 7). Paul all but discourages speculation on the nature of the "risen body" (1 Cor 15, 35). He answers the Corinthians in a series of negatives: the resurrected body will not be like the conditions of our present existence, namely "perishable", "dishonourable", "weak", "physical", but, through the transformative power of the Spirit, imperishable, glorious, powerful, spiritual. . . . He seems concerned to liberate hope so that it can be open to its proper level of mystery, the power of the divine Spirit to bring about a fulfilment "far more abundantly than anything we can ask or think" (Eph 3,20). Even if one rightly supposes that the single clear matter is God and his love, such certainties of faith are not held in the security of any earthly mode of knowing: the end will come "at the proper time . . . manifest by the Lord of Lords and the King of Kings, who alone has immortality and dwells in unapproachable light, whom no man has seen or can see" (1 Tim 6, 16). The mystery of Heaven is always hidden within the abiding mystery of God.

Spirit-inspired hope will not allow the Heaven of our final

existence to be reduced to any category within the present sphere of our experience. It seems that hope blossoms to its proper "theological" proportion by being left in the dark. Thus, it is to our "advantage" that Jesus "goes away", to make room, as it were, for the proper creativity of hope through the inspiration of the Spirit . . . "otherwise the Paraclete will not come to you. But if I go, I will send him to you" (Jn 16,7). He will declare "the things that are to come" (Jn 16,13).

Failure to observe this scriptural way of thinking has resulted in trivialising the mystery of Heaven. Our very human impatience with the "unknowing" character of true hope ("hope that is seen is not hope. Who hopes for what he sees?" Rom 8,24) has fixated and congealed the dynamic images and symbols of Heaven in such a way as to provoke, not an anticipation of life's fullness, but almost a dissatisfaction with what appears to be a diminished, inactive shadow existence for separated souls.

Nonetheless, however "unknowing" our hope is, Christian existence "groans" for an all-liberating fulfilment. The whole of creation groans in some great process of giving birth, in eager longing for the revelation of the sons of God, in the hope "that it will be set free from its bondage to decay and obtain the glorious liberty of the children of God" (Rom 8, 18-22). Within that creation groaning for its fulfilment, "we ourselves groan inwardly" for the full evidence of what we are called to be (v. 23). Then the Holy Spirit, whose first fruits we possess, assists us, in the darkness and vulnerability of our hopes, interceding for us with "unutterable groanings" (v. 26).[4]

So, creation groans for its final liberation. Within that creation, Christians groan for the fulfilment of their hope. Within Christians, as the inspiration and support of their hope, the Spirit groans in what we must take as a divine compassion for all creation searching for its point of home-coming, expanding hope to a horizon that only God and his Christ can fill.

4. Heaven in Christ:

To insist on hope's "unknowing", to stress the limitlessness of the horizon of Christian hope, might appear to leave the notion of Heaven without much content at all. Nonetheless, within such a *theologia negativa* and against this limitless horizon, we can appreciate more fully one absolutely central datum: Jesus Christ, the Incarnate Word, crucified and risen. Heaven is the ultimate dimension of everything that Christ is.

In a variety of ways, the New Testament elaborates the mystery of Christ, and at least implicitly suggests an ultimacy which is fundamental for our understanding of Heaven.[5] So often the Christian Scriptures present Jesus as the fulfilment of all previous dispensations (e.g. Hb 1, 1f). This language of fulfilment looks to a consummation when all things will be subjected to him, including the "last enemy", death (1 Cor 15, 20-29).

Related to this there is another type of language: only by participating in his Spirit, his life, his death, his resurrection, do we, who follow him, have life and find our way to the Father. This, too, suggests an ultimate fulfilment: "If the Spirit of him who raised Jesus from the dead dwells in you . . . he will give life to your mortal bodies also" (Rom 8, 11).

Another remarkable arc of Christological meaning, is the effort to englobe "all things" — the totality of the cosmos — in the mystery of Christ: all things were created "in him", "through him", "for him". He is the coherence and consistency of creation (Col 1, 15ff). This is conceived at once as "in the beginning" and as a state of ultimate being, "a plan for the fullness of time to unite all things in him, things in heaven and things on earth" (Eph 1,10).

In each of these ways of thinking, Christ is the central defining point, as it were, of Heaven. He is the fulfilment of human history. He is the Life in which we live. He is the ultimate coherence of the universe in which we exist.

From each of these points of view, Christ is the essential focus of the meaning of Heaven. It is not so much that Christ is "in Heaven" as that Heaven is being "in Christ". He is God's parable of "what God has prepared for those who love him". His death contests any self-enclosed worldly version of life. His resurrection frees hope to anticipate a final dimension of life as a new creation in the Spirit. His cosmic significance, comprising all things, invites the believer to envisage a final coherence and consistency of reality in him. He is "the Life" (Jn 14,6), one who has come "that you might have life and have it to the full" (Jn 10,10).

It is important to focus the meaning of Heaven in the reality of Christ. Detached from the personal, concrete "Living One" (Rev 1, 18), theology is at the mercy of a lush apocalyptic symbolism. This may say more about the dynamics of "wish-fulfilment" than about the movement of hope which is based on fidelity to the Crucified, with the love and service that this entails.

As a parable of the "Life" of Heaven, Jesus embodies both the "Truth" of God and the "Way" of our approach to the Father. Heaven is the final revelation of God and the fulfilment of human life. A word, then, on each of these aspects.

5. The Heaven of God:

Heaven is the God incarnate in Jesus, communicated and revealed. If "God was in Christ reconciling the world to himself" (2 Cor 5, 19), Heaven is the culmination of this divine activity in regard to creation. It is that fulfilment of divine Love reaching beyond itself in the incarnation and in the outpouring of the Spirit, to enfold the world explicitly into the reality from which it always lived, and in which it always existed.[6]

In this theocentric horizon, Heaven must be understood as the definitive Reign of God, the mystery of God's presence which Jesus announced and made present. In another idiom (e.g. Karl Rahner) it is the achievement of God's self-communication, "the immeasurable greatness of his power working within us" (Eph 2, 19) finally revealed.

These assertions add up to one thing. Heaven, first of all, is God coming into his own. It is the divine Mystery, revealed in Jesus, finally made explicit. So, before theology speaks in terms of human fulfilment, Heaven is fundamentally a divine fulfilment: Merciful Love finally unfolded; the Son subsuming the whole of creation into his relationship with the Father; the Spirit penetrating and possessing the universe as a field of divine communication and love.

This is to suggest that Heaven is, in the first place, the Trinity "enworlded", or, if you prefer, the world "trinified": the whole of creation is enfolded into the love-life of Father, Son and Holy Spirit. Heaven is primarily God's Heaven, a divine infinite Joy in self-giving, in the ecstasy of being "everything to everyone" (1 Cor 15,28).

If then Jesus is the personal focus of what Heaven might mean, its fundamental pole of reference is to God, not God finally attained, but God finally triumphant in his self-giving love. To bring such a Heaven into being, God has to overcome the resistance of creation to the life and communion which he is. He does this in a mercy which both disarms and heals, by giving what is most intimate to himself, his Son and Spirit, into the God-less places of creation. The process culminates in a world entirely transfigured by the divine presence and completely receptive to the divine gift. So, before Heaven is our vision of God, it must be God's delight in us.

Although this divine dynamic of self-giving is a fundamental, it is a notion without flesh and blood unless it is anchored in the meaning of Christ and in our human concerns for life and "life to the full" which Jesus came to give (Jn 10, 10).

We turn, then, to that other pole of the meaning of Heaven, human existence brought to fulfilment.

6. Heaven as the Fullness of Life:

The life of Christ as the Risen One implies that the Heavenly mode of existence does not mean a return to this present form of earthly life. That would make it merely a resuscitation for endless, and pointless, longevity. That may be the implicit longing of the beauty parlour and the health studio and, occasionally, of the intensive care unit. But that is not the Christian meaning of eternal life. Yet neither is it the negation of the contradiction of what we call life in the key moments of our experience. After all, the resurrection is the transformation, not the destruction of the crucified Jesus. The resurrection, as a central symbol of the life of Heaven, does not imply the negation of our identity, our freedom, our values, our life-shaping commitments. This was what Oscar Romero saw with dramatic clarity. Though it certainly looks to the future for its flowering and fruitfulness (". . . It has not yet appeared what we shall be" 1 Jn 3,2), it is already germinating and sprouting in the vigour of our present following of Christ: "We know we have passed from death to life because we love the brethren. He who does not love, remains in death" (1 Jn 3,14). What, then, are the seeds of this eternal life of Heaven already planted in the earth of our existence?[7]

They are, of course, "as large as life": here, I will mention just three ways of identifying the kind of life that looks to Heavenly fulfilment. First, Heaven as the resurrection of the body; secondly, Heaven as the fulfilment of love and relationships; thirdly, Heaven as the vision of God.

7. The Resurrection of the Body:

Heaven is the resurrection of the body. The Risen Lord is not disembodied; he is not a "separated soul" more or less haunting the world (See Lk 24,36-43). He has entered into a newly embodied existence. Into this, he draws those who believe in him (1 Cor 15,12-27). The sacraments are signs of this new Spiritual embodiment.

Admittedly, there are problems about the meaning of the body, given the complexities of the scriptural and philosophical terminology in this area. If it happens that one thinks of death as the soul's release from the prison of the body (a classical Greek position), it is no great consolation to be reimprisoned for all eternity! Christian tradition, founding itself on a more biblical manner of thinking and availing itself of a more positive philosophy of soul-body relationship, and by the very thrust of its sacramental practice, has usually been far more positive about the body. As I said above, after all, the resurrection of Jesus does not mean the destruction of his humanity.[8]

A general Christian philosophical position would go something like this: there can be no soul unless it is intrinsically related to an embodied material existence. For to be human is to be, from different points of view, both an animated body, and an embodied soul. Through the body, the human spirit is present to a world and functions within it. In that deep sense, it is through the body that we exist and belong to the world: we are embodied in time, space, relationships, "here" as an individual recognisable entity within the world. We not only *have* bodies, but *are* bodies, a *somebody,* in, with and for a world. Teilhard de Chardin remarked that human embodiment means not so much that we possess part of the world totally, but that we possess the whole of the world partially.[9]

To exist as a human being, even as a spiritual being, means to be embodied in the "matter" of the world. The soul exists and functions in what is other than itself, so to become embodied in the ensemble of relationships, dynamics, conditions we understand as "our world". To have a body means to have a world, to be intrinsically part of a larger whole.

If then Christian hope expresses itself in terms of the resurrection of the body, it is not longing for a resuscitation in this little bit of exchangeable matter. It is envisaging a complete embodiment in that world which is radically God's creation, which comes to us and bears us on in all the patient unfolding of the cosmos and in all the varied forms of human creativity. Such a hope does not want to escape from its essential world but to belong completely, creatively to it.

For, from such a world, our human spirits have drawn life and sustenance. In it, we have found beauty and felt the breadth of human belonging. Within it, we have touched upon the mystery of our origin and our end. In its history, we have met the Christ. Into such a world we die, to make the earth more fruitful and hallowed for future generations. Hence to hope for the resurrection of the body implies a cosmic hope: that we are saved with and in our world.

Modern science is suggesting the incredible extent to which

194

this material creation was wedded, right from the first moment of its existence, to the emergence of human life. From one point of view, it seems, when one looks at the conditions operative within the twenty thousand million years of evolution, that human existence is an event of almost zero-probability. It could all have been so different. Yet it wasn't. This material universe has groaned onward in a kind of amazing love-affair with us human beings that have come into being at this late stage, this last few hundred thousand years.[10]

The cosmos has toiled through these thousands of millions of years to bring forth our human present. In our human consciousness, the vast impersonal past and the vision of a personal future meet in the joy of recognition. For this material world continues to give itself to us to be our food, our drink, our breath. It offers its energies to be tapped for the human good. We live out of it and die back into it.

In the minds of our great thinkers, it has become a universe present to itself as an immeasurable wonder. To the inspiration of our artists, it offers its shapes and colours, its sounds and movements, to burst forth into ever new forms. In our mystics, it comes to know itself as something holy, a vast sacred site alive with an all-personal Mystery. In human science and craft, it yields itself to human use, no longer a blind force threatening human kind, but a resource nurturing the emergence of a global humanity. It has become, as it were, the shared body of the human spirit.

In such a vision, the cosmos and the human spirit interact to bring into being what we recognise as our human world. The human spirit finds its proper place in a material world. And this material world is lifted to new levels of being through the activity of the human mind and heart and hand. For the Word to have become flesh, to remain eternally human, means that he has possessed this world as his own. Already in him, it has become the beginning of a new creation. Neither for the New Adam nor for us who believe in him, can Heaven mean leaving this world behind. It must mean this world, and ourselves in it, brought to fulfilment. All the "groaning" we referred to above, will yield to the "Alleluia" of a creation finally at home with its Creator.

Vatican II did not refrain from expressing this cosmic dimension of human hope when, to give one instance, it stated, "with death conquered, the children of God will be raised in Christ, and what is sown in weakness and dishonour will put on the imperishable: charity and its works remain, and all of creation which God made for Man, will be set free from its bondage to decay" (*Gaudium et Spes,* No. 39).

Heaven, then, as the resurrection of the body, means life in a world transformed; a transformed world in which we are newly embodied.

8. Heaven as Love:

Heaven is not only the complete "incarnation" or embodiment of our existence in Christ. It is the final liberation of the heart. The life of Heaven is one of unrestricted being-in-love.

What we experience as our "real life" is most of all our loves, our relationships — everything we conscientiously give ourselves to. Oscar Romero knew this: his life was, above everything else, his commitment to his people. Heaven, as he understood it, far from being the negation of this commitment, was his "rising again in the people of El Salvador": "If God accepts the sacrifice of my life, then may my blood be the seed of liberty, and a sign of hope that will soon become a reality". (*Excelsior* interview of Note 2). It is entirely in accord with the logic of faith and hope to envisage Heaven as the fulfilment of the fundamental passion of our existence to be for others. It is what is called a "Pro-existence", the complete expansion for our earthly loves and service, into the sphere of the Spirit. "Love remains" (1 Cor 13, 8).

Jesus, the crucified and Risen One, is the form of the new creation. Those who believe in him to the point of following him in the kind of life he lived, united with him in the kind of death he died, wake, in him, to a fully relational existence, an existence amplified to be totally "for God" and "all in

God". All our authentic loves and commitments, be they sexual, familial, social, global, are redeemed and liberated to an unambiguous and complex scope. Heaven is a fully relational existence, the sphere of complete belonging and compassion in all the dimensions of Spirit of Christ. Yves Congar quotes from a notebook of Dostoievsky in a way that illumines this point:

> To love somebody else as one loves oneself, which Christ told us to do, — that is impossible. We are bound by the force of earthly personality: the "me" stands in the way. Christ, and Christ alone, did it; but he was the eternal ideal, the ideal of the ages, to which man aspires and must aspire, impelled by nature.
>
> Nevertheless, since Christ came to earth as man's ideal in the flesh, it has become clear as daylight what the last and highest stage of the evolution of the personality must be. It is this: when his evolving is finished, at the very point where the end is reached, man finds out . . . with all the force of his nature that the highest use he can make of his personality, of the full flowering of his *self,* is to do away with it, to give it wholly to any and everybody, without division or reserve. And that is sovereign happiness. Thus, the law of "me" is fused with the law of mankind; and the "I" and "all" (in appearance two opposite extremes) each suppressing itself for the sake of the other, reach the highest peak of their individual development, each one separately.
>
> This is exactly the paradise that Christ offers. The whole history of mankind, and of each individual man and woman, is simply an evolution towards and an aspiration to, struggle for, and achievement of this end.[11]

Nowhere is Augustine's axiom, "Show me a lover and he will understand", more applicable. This is what Romero grasped. It remains the hope of every martyr.

9. Heaven as the Vision of God:

The classical Thomist doctrine of the "Beatific Vision" and even its ecclesiastical formulation in "Benedictus Deus"

197

(1336) and in the Council of Florence (1439) seem very intellectual. To "enjoy the divine essence in an intuitive vision" might give the impression that Heaven is primarily for theologians. However, the final vision of the Divine Essence is more surely intimated in the ordinary experiences of life — in contrast to the more abstract struggle of the theologian with his problems. In every life (therefore, not *excluding* theologians) there are inklings of what might be described as a final vision. Already we obscurely recognise an ultimate all-welcoming truth. The poets, especially if they are mystics as well, most of all testify to this: when "the egg-shell collapses in the fist of the eternal instant" (R. G. Fitzgerald); when we sense "the dearest freshness deep down things" (Hopkins); when, with Wordsworth, we waken to "the presence which disturbs with the joy of elevated thoughts". Then, there are experiences such as that described in Belloc's *The Path to Rome*. The author has his first glimpse of the Alps:

> Their sharp steadfastness and their clean uplifted lines compelled my adoration. Up there, the sky above and below them, part of the sky but part of us, the great peaks made communion with that homing creeping part of me which loves vineyards and dances and a slow movement among pastures, and that other part which is only properly at home in Heaven. I say that this kind of description is useless, and that it is better to address prayers to such things than to attempt to interpret them for others. . . .
>
> Since I could now see such a wonder and it could work such things in my mind, therefore, some day, I should be part of it. That is what I felt.[12]

Some kind of final vision is intimated in the extraordinary movements of ordinary life: peak-experiences, inklings, presentiments, foreshadowings of the true face of God. How, concretely, this occurs can only be suggested in each one's personal experience as each of us might come to detect such moments in the love we have read in the beauty of a human face; in the sudden impact of natural splendour; the release of mind following an insight into a perplexing problem; the glory of the stars in the inland sky; the resonance of great music; the arresting quality of all great art . . . the primordial magic of Spring after a long Winter. . . .

What are these moments when all of us have seen something? In such glimpses, we sense that we are made for some final vision. We know, in an uncanny inner evidence, that we are on the edge of something; that a limitlessly wonderful Beyond has smiled upon us, in the fleeting limited moments of ordinary life.

Only occasionally, perhaps, and always with a certain distance and non-possession; but enough to recognise our homeland, the *patria,* where shines the eternal light that has already dimly touched us. Now "through a glass darkly, but then, face to face" (1 Cor 12, 13).

Such a final vision will be at once the joy of complete evidence, God explicit; and the beginning of an endless adventure, God always infinite even as the Mystery reveals itself. . . .

Conclusion:

Heaven is the ultimate language of hope.[13] Such a hope is not incompatible with our dark familiarity with malice and pain, within and beyond us. Our generation is not inexperienced in such things. But even that is made bearable by our hope in the Risen One, Heaven in person. It brings us to the conviction that true life cannot be extinguished; that it will come into its own in a world transformed, in a love set free to expand to its fullest proportion, in the evidence of the final Mystery.

In that hope, even as we accept the finitude and vulnerability of even the best among us, such as Oscar Romero, a daring, defiant, persistent joy is renewed, to leave us with only one real question: if true life lasts, why not live now?

1. Quoted in Hans Küng, *Eternal Life,* Doubleday: New York, 1984, pg. 198.
2. Originally from an interview with *Excelsior* of Mexico City.
3. See Küng, *op. cit.,* 44-68; 176-200.

4. I am indebted to Brendan Byrne, SJ, for calling my attention to these "groanings", as for much else in this reflection. See his "Life After Death", *ACR* 49/4 (Oct 1982, 386-403).

5. See G. Mattelet, *L'Au-dela Retrouvé, Christologie des fins dernières.* Desclee: Paris 1975.

6. P. Duckworth, "Hope For Heaven", *Compass* 18 (Autumn) 1984, 19-23. Especially the section *God's Communication in Grace,* pg. 20.

7. See the excellent suggestions in Duckworth, *op. cit.* on this whole area. Also J. Wilken, SJ, "Life After Death: Theological Views", *Compass* (Spring) 1982, 29-41. This is a very useful and well-situated survey of classical and modern theological views.

8. Brendan Byrne in *op. cit.,* pg. 399ff, nicely summarises the Pauline meaning of *Soma.*

9. The whole passage reads: "My own body is not these cells or those cells that *belong exclusively* to me. It is *what* in these cells *and* in the rest of the world, feels my influence and reacts against me. *My* matter is not a part of the universe that I possess *totaliter;* it is the *Totality* of the universe possessed by me *partialiter".* In *Science and Christ,* Collins: London, 1968, pg. 13.

10. See the fascinating points made by Prof. Mark Doughty in his articles in *The Tablet* (Aug 28 and Sept 4, 1982).

11. Quoted in *The Wide World My Parish*, Darton, Longman and Todd: London, 1967, pg. 60f.

12. Pp. 180f of the Allen and Unwin edition of 1949.

13. My own article in *Compass* 18, Autumn 1984, 1-4, "The Last Things" gives a more general view of our eschatological hope.